Do You Really Need To Write A Book?

Tips & Techniques for Writing,
Publishing, Marketing & Promoting
YOUR BOOK!

Do You Really Need To Write A Book?

Tips & Techniques for Writing,
Publishing, Marketing & Promoting
YOUR BOOK!

Carol Adler, MFA

Dandelion Books, LLC
www.dandelion-books.com

Do You Really Need To Write A Book?

© Copyright, 2009 by Carol Adler

All rights exclusively reserved. No part of this book may be reproduced or translated into any language or utilized in any form or by any means, electronic or mechanical, including photocopying, recording or by any information storage and retrieval system, without permission in writing from the publisher.

Dandelion Books, LLC, Mesa, Arizona, United States of America

Adler, Carol
    Do You Really Need To Write A Book? Tips & Techniques for Writing, Publishing, Marketing & Promoting YOUR BOOK!

ISBN 978-1-934280-78-2
LC Number 2009941558

Cover & Book Design by Colin Dunbar http://www.colindunbar.com

Disclaimer and Reader Agreement

Under no circumstances will the publisher, Dandelion Books, LLC, or author be liable to any person or business entity for any direct, indirect, special, incidental, consequential, or other damages based on any use of this book or any other source to which it refers, including, without limitation, any lost profits, business interruption, or loss of programs or information.

Reader Agreement for Accessing This Book

By reading this book, you, the reader, consent to bear sole responsibility for your own decisions to use or read any of this book's material. Dandelion Books, LLC and the author shall not be liable for any damages or costs of any type arising out of any action taken by you or others based upon reliance on any materials in this book.

Other Books by Carol Adler

Non-Fiction
How To Publish & Market a Book Without Jumping Off a Cliff (ebook) http://www.dandelion-books.com/publish-it.html

Write to Publish for Profit (ebook) http://www.dandelion-books.com/write-to-publish-for-profit.html

Fiction
Come as You Are (by Sarah Daniels, a pseudonym) (hard copy & ebook)

Slouching Past Bethlehem (hard copy and ebook) http://www.dandelion-books.com/Dandelion-Downloads.html

The Woman With Qualities (by Sarah Daniels, a pseudonym) (hard copy & ebook)

Poetry
Arioso – Selected Poems by Carol Adler (ebook) http://www.dandelion-books.com/poetry-self-publishing.html

Jesus & The Tooth Fairy – Poems by Carol Adler (ebook) http://www.dandelion-books.com/Jesus-and-the-tooth-fairy.html

Naked in Daylight (ebook) http://www.dandelion-books.com/naked-in-dayhlight.html

Do You Really Need To Write A Book?

"Read, every day, something no one else is reading. Think, every day, something no one else is thinking. Do, every day, something no one else would be silly enough to do. It is bad for the mind to continually be part of unanimity."

—Gotthold Ephraim Lessing (1729-1781)
German Dramatist

"Everything we shut our eyes to, everything we run away from, everything we deny, denigrate or despise, serves to defeat us in the end. What seems nasty, painful, evil, can become a source of beauty, joy, and strength, if faced with an open mind."

—Henry Miller (1891-1980)
American writer

*"Go on a journey from self to Self, my friend...
Such a journey transforms the earth into a mine of gold."*

—Jalal-ud-Din Rumi (1207-1273)
Persian poet

Do You Really Need To Write A Book?

To my clients, who continue to be my best teachers.

∞

A special thanks to Perry Mardon, http://www.mardoninternational.com, for inviting me to send him one of my books to add to his amazing product list.

Do You Really Need To Write A Book?

Contents

Introduction 1
1 The 5 W's, Starting with Who 5
2 Horton's Who 13
3 Why Do I Need a Book? 25
4 The Big How 33
5 Should I Contract a Ghostwriter or Book Doctor? 49
6 Publishing & Promoting Your Book 61
7 Bottom Line 87
8 More About Marketing Your Books Online 101
I'm Here for You 115
About the Author 117
Testimonials from Carol's Clients 119

Introduction

Sooner or later, someone—your business coach, marketing director, mentor, significant other, mother, mother-in-law, astrologer, etc.—is going to tell you that you need to write a book.

"But I'm not a writer," you protest. "I don't even know where to begin!"

Or: "I'd *love* to find time to write a book. I'd also like to find time to go to my son's Little League games, take in the new show at the Art Museum, learn how to tango, and—"

Or you might come back with a simple: "Why? Why do I need to write a book?"

Meaning, *I've got enough headaches. Why should I add yet another one?*

The message is clear. I get it, and I can see it: Mr. or Ms. Entrepreneur dashing out to the car port, one jacket sleeve dangling, hair brush in teeth, cell phone ringing… writing a book is simply out of the question.

Your time is budgeted down to the nth minute. In addition to managing your staff, overseeing business operations and making executive decisions, you really want to take a more active part in the community; family life suffers more than you care to admit... and you never seem to get caught up either at home or at the office.

Some highly successful business people have yet another reason for not writing a book. They'll candidly admit that if not for their Dream Team of administrative assistants, they could never compose even the simplest staff memo. It is a fact that often highly successful business people are terrible spellers, know next to nothing about grammar and freak out every time they're asked to write a simple letter. Some have never even graduated from high school.

Another challenge may be lack of computer skills. A book may seem out of the question except possibly through dictation or interviews captured on a recording machine and transcribed.

And yet... if you ask any professional on the career track, they'll be quick to tell you that **having a published book is essential.** If you give workshops and seminars, in addition to providing a product for back of the room sales, **a book serves as a glorified business card.** It is part of your Professional Package, your Promotional Tool Kit.

Introduction

Ghostwriters and book doctors to the rescue

In many businesses and professions, ghostwriters, book doctors and editors have become an integral part of the company's staff. And now with the arrival of blogging, social networking, article posting and other online forms of communication, good writers and editors are in even greater demand.

Sometimes gifts arrive when least expected. I had just electronically delivered a package of edited documents to Perry Mardon http://www.mardoninternational.com who is a highly successful business man—the kind of professional with clearly defined goals and determination to deliver the best of himself at all times (my kind of person!). In Perry's email confirming that he'd received the documents, he wrote that he'd like to promote one of my products. Did I have a book that would fit into his product line?

That was all the encouragement I needed to start developing a new work that would complement Perry's business coaching enterprise.

This is my third book about writing and publishing,* but it is the first time I have chosen to develop a work specifically for entrepreneurs and other professionals.

By the time you finish reading this book, I hope you will agree that a published book bearing your byline is a necessity, as important to your business as recruiting and training a competent staff, tracking sales leads, analyzing campaign successes and failures, and maintaining an excellent customer relations department.

In the long run, writing a book or having it written for you is a small investment in time, energy and money compared to both the tangible and intangible returns. In addition to new business leads and enhanced branding, you will experience the rewards of recognition from people who thought they knew who you were and what you stood for, but who now view you with even greater understanding, respect and admiration.

Another built-in bonus that by itself is more than enough reason for you to write a book: ultimately you will discover that by sharing yourself with others you'll end up getting to know yourself even better. That self-knowledge, to paraphrase Perry Mardon's words, is exactly what is required to transform you from a "just okay" business leader and manager to a great one.

*My first book on writing, *Write to Publish for Profit*, is a how-to manual for the general public, with a section about writing to publish for profit. The second book, *How to Publish & Market a Book without Jumping off a Cliff*, is a how-to manual that addresses specific publishing and marketing issues. Both are available as downloads through http://www.dandelion-books.com and Amazon Kindle.

1

The 5 W's, Starting with Who

Today's marketplace is flooded with books: old ones, new ones, out-of-print ones and newly reissued ones; fiction, non-fiction, poetry; books on every subject for every age group. There are even books written by dogs to be read to their owners. (I happen to know about this particular subject because I was asked to edit and publish one.) I'm sure other species in the animal kingdom have also authored books.

You: If so many books on every subject imaginable are already out there, **why should I or anyone else write another one?** Haven't we reached the saturation point?

Me: Difficult questions deserve easy answers. Simply because a book you write will be yours. Your book that will be the "Hi-5 W + 1 H" that is you: the Who-What-Where-When-Why & How of the person who answers to your name, physical description, birth date and place, etc., etc.

You: You mean The **Who** That I Am is so incredibly different from other people's "who's" that's it's actually worthy of a book?

Me: You bet it is! Don't sell yourself short. And incidentally, speaking of selling, that's what this is all about. As a business owner, entrepreneur or professional who offers products and services, by now you've learned that business—and life—are all about networking or sharing: informing, inspiring, enlightening, entertaining, and telling stories. Your business is your story. And so is a book that bears your byline. Both tell the world who you are and what you're all about.

Your book is also about success

You probably know by now that the key to success is doing what you love, loving what you do, and finding a way to support yourself in the process. A person who loves nature—hiking and camping, for example, may decide to become a forest ranger. If they also love animals, they may start an exotic animal farm. A person who loves to play the violin may decide to become a concert violinist, violin teacher or orchestral player.

You: Okay, so I do love what I do. You're right about that. And I do it well. I'm an auto mechanic and I have a repair shop in the medium-size town where I live. Now let's get back to the book idea. Why do I need to write a book?

Me: You don't. You don't have to do anything in this world that you don't want to! You really don't have to share your passion for fixing vehicles—I happen to know that you're also a collector. You have some vintage cars that you're mighty proud of! (Your eyes start to sparkle.)

I wonder if you have some tips you'd like to share with other folks who love cars as much as you do. How did you get started? Did you have to go to school to earn a degree or did you learn by figuring things out for yourself? I bet you've got some interesting stories about those first years working for other mechanics, and then making the decision to open your own shop.

You: Well... I did have some pretty crazy things happen. For a while there one time, during the recession I was wondering how I was going to survive. But I learned some pretty neat tricks about helping folks out and making it a win/win for everyone. You know, I've got this incredible '59 Cadillac Convertible 62-S...

Me: I think you're catching on! Believe me, every business owner, every entrepreneur and every professional, has a story.

Several years ago, a 59-year-old world champion martial artist who specialized in *tai kwan do*, contacted me. "I've got a great rejuvenation program," he told me. "Imagine at my age, I'm a world champion. I'm still as strong and agile as I was thirty years ago!"

"I want to share my health and fitness program with the world," he said excitedly. "I want everyone to know how I stay fit. It's a mind-body thing. Most people don't know that."

I was listening carefully. The all-important "who" was a man who had made a name for himself; he was known the world over for his martial arts achievements at an age when people are supposed to be physically on the decline.

The "what" was a rejuvenation program: this man's personal fitness regime that he felt he could duplicate and restructure or customize to work for people of all ages and backgrounds, athletic or not.

The "where" was anywhere he could find a listening or reading public, and the "when" was now. Get the book written now. The "why" was obvious. This man was inspired and he wanted to motivate others. He was passionate about helping people live longer and better and showing them how to make the most of every minute of their lives.

He had only one problem. His education had stopped after eighth grade. So he'd come to me, asking me if I would write his book for him.

What an honor! Because this high achiever was determined to make it happen, he'd found an investor to pay for having me ghostwrite his book, and also for setting up a rejuvenation company. He would be the manager and spokesperson for the company, I would direct the publishing division, and we would hire a marketing and promotion director.

Ultimately, the book became his entrance to the local and regional fitness world where he conducted seminars and demonstrations. His target market covered a large demographic group. In addition to the health and fitness crowd ranging from teens to seniors, his program and book attracted martial artists as well as the retired "snowbird" group in the Florida area where he lived. They especially loved the *tai chi* classes he installed in the various seniors' communities up and down the Florida coast. He sold books everywhere and even started to do a series of rejuvenation cruise seminars.

As he continued to compete, he won yet another world championship during the year the book was published. Eventually he added more products, including an excellent line of *tai chi* DVDs. In addition to his martial arts career, he launched two other businesses through the publishing of his book.

What's your story?

Let's say you like to create video games. Maybe you got a degree as an engineer or one in computer technology. You decided to take a job with a toy manufacturer and you invented a new game, got it patented and opened up your own company.

You have a story.

Maybe you like to take photos. You trained at one of the many outstanding schools that teach digital graphics technologies. You started your own photography business, specializing in family portraits and creating digital family albums, "womb to tomb." You have a story.

Maybe you're a runner who decided to train for the Olympics. You took a job at a health club as a fitness trainer and set to work practicing. Competition was stiff, but you made the team!

How did you do it? What were your successes? Your failures? What would you like to share with others that you feel is one of the most important things you've learned so far (the "take-away")?

Let's review that original list of objections to writing your book and let me add a few more that I hear often:

- I don't have time.

- I don't like to write.
- I don't even know how to write paragraph; how could I ever write a book?
- I wouldn't even know where to begin.
- What do I really have to say that's different from what's already out there in the marketplace, that's been said over... and over... and over...?
- Who's going to buy my book besides family, friends, relatives and a few business associates?
- I already know how difficult it would be to find a literary agent to shop my book to a publisher; this may take months, even years. And by then, my book is already outdated. We're living in a rapid transition society.
- If I did find a publisher that was interested in signing a contract with me, how much money would I really make? I've heard horror stories about publishers' contracts and royalties.
- Yes, I could self-publish... but that can be expensive. And if it's done cheaply through one of the on line turnkey companies, I've heard other horror stories about their "finished books." Surely in the world of business, one of those so-called "fast food" products wouldn't stand up to a quality book that is expertly edited, proofed and taken through each stage of production with special consideration for the look and feel as well as the content.

Although I've already touched on the first few of these issues, in the following chapters, I'll give all of them a fair chance on the witness stand.

First, however, I want to tell you about an email I received the other day from a man who recently retired from a successful career as a surgeon. He has decided to make writing his next full-time career.

His reason: "I have always felt that writing something down makes it real."

In other words, nothing was "real" to this man unless he put it in writing. Everything he'd done, all of his accomplishments were merely whispers of a memory, "gone with the wind" unless he picked up a pen and pad or sat down at his computer keyboard and captured them with his words.

Perhaps that email best describes the most important reason for anyone to write a book. **Writing is a validation process.** You validate yourself or confirm your identity to yourself when you actually express or "export" your thoughts and feelings from your mind and heart and impress or "import" them to paper or the computer screen.

You: I have a feeling you're twisting my arm.
Me: Me? Why would I want to do that?!

2
Horton's Who

Following is another story I want to share with you that was told to me by a good friend and colleague, also a writer and editor.

"I'm married to an amazing man," she told me, "and he has an amazing story." I knew that her husband, "Tim," was a well-known artist. His works could be found in most of the permanent collections of major art museums throughout the world.

"One day," continued my friend, "I suggested to Tim that he write his memoirs and he responded, as I knew he would, "But I'm not a writer. I'm a painter! You're the writer. Why don't you write them for me?"

"That's all the encouragement I needed—and in fact, that's probably what I wanted him to say! I'd already created an MP3 file on my computer for collecting the interviews with him that I would transcribe and turn into a book.

"We had a wonderful time doing the recording sessions because it gave us a chance to reminisce about the many years we'd spent together. His childhood was also very dramatic. His parents were dairy farmers from the Midwest and neither of them understood or appreciated their youngest son's passion to become an artist. It's an amazing, bittersweet story how he ran away from home, hiding as a stowaway on a freight train and ending up in Chicago where he earned money painting signs and houses… eventually winning a scholarship to the Chicago Art Institute. It's a real American rags to riches story!

"Upon completing the draft of Tim's autobiography, I shared it with an editor colleague for her input, but when I received her comments a short time later, I was devastated as well as extremely disappointed.

"Here's what she wrote:

> Dear M,
>
> You did such a great job! You're such a good writer. BUT… I have to be totally honest with you. Otherwise I couldn't live with myself, and we're close enough that I know you'll understand exactly what I mean.
>
> Tim isn't in this book. He's had such an extraordinary life and his stories are magical. But the reader never really learns about him. We never discover the inner monologue, what he's thinking and feeling throughout all these experiences. In other words, it's all about the stories and not about Tim.

What are his deepest thoughts, his feelings, his dreams? How does he feel about such and such? When such and such happened to him, how did he react inwardly? What did he learn from it?

When he paints, what inner process does he go through? Is the preparation easy or difficult? Is it different every time he starts a new work? What are his deepest fears?

I think you know what I mean. A man's *life* is here through these anecdotes—and so skillfully written. But the *man himself is absent.* That's the most important part of a biography... the part people really want to identify with. What does he really want to tell the reader about himself?

"I showed the letter to my husband, waiting for a response to register in his eyes, his facial expression, his body language.

"Nothing. Nothing at all except a shrug of his shoulders and a secret smile. 'You see,' he said at length, 'that's the point.'

"'What do you mean, "that's the point?"' I asked him, not understanding.

"'I'm an artist, not a writer. I paint. Whatever I have to tell the world is in my paintings—and if people don't understand, if they don't get it—that's *their* problem, not mine. My message to the world is in my art, not in a book.'

"I understood what he was saying, yet deep down, I didn't totally agree with him. It's not that he's so much more than his painting because *his art is who he is.* And his message is powerful. If it doesn't move you or 'get you in the gut,' he feels as though he's failed to communicate, to express himself. That communication or expression for him is not through the written word and a published book, but through his paintings.

"Yes, I certainly did understand," my friend continued, "even though I wasn't satisfied. I still felt empty. Certainly no artist needs to be called to the witness stand to defend themselves, to explain 'what their work means' or 'what they're trying to say.' I was after something different. First and foremost, Tim expresses himself through the medium of painting, the visual arts. He is also a person, and even though the two are integrally linked, he also has the ability, as we all do, to be self-reflective, to view himself as the 'observer,' or as he appears as a Self to himself."

My editor friend was trying to explain the difference between a book written by an artist, and the artist's output. It's true that often a creative person also discovers another form of self-validation through a written version of their memoirs.

You: That really is an interesting story, and I have to admit, I'm not a particularly modest person. I do have a high regard for myself, but let's be honest. A new book has to be original. What would make people want to read and buy my book?

Me: Thank you! That is exactly the question I've been waiting for you to ask so I could deliver the meat and potatoes of this book.

2 – Horton's Who

Let's not waste another minute! My message to you can be summed up in six little words:

> You are your most important asset.

Those six words are your Treasure, your Gold Mine. They include your self-esteem and your self-love. They inspire and motivate you to be the very best you can be at all times, 24/7, whether in the work place, at home, giving a seminar, socializing…

When you believe in yourself and value yourself as your greatest asset, you know you have no other choice than to "go for the gold." No holds barred. And that's why you need to write a book—because you have a **wealth of material** to share with others.

Your Journey

After getting your degrees or certification for engaging in your chosen endeavor, you started your apprenticeship with the masters. Either you were employed somewhere and worked your way up through the ranks, or you served as an intern for an already established professional.

At a certain point you felt you were ready to "leave home" and start your own business or launch your career. As you proceeded to build the foundation for your new enterprise, you began to formulate your own ideas about what works and what doesn't. You also started to develop new strategies for adapting to changing times. You soon learned that the field was wide open for experimentation because technology is changing faster than most people can keep up with it.

Your Mission

If you are a skillful, savvy leader, you make a commitment to stay on top of the latest and greatest innovations. No time could ever be more exciting than now, and you're bursting with ideas. You can't wait to start doing things *your way.*

You may have even come to the point where you disagree with some of your teachers. Also, what worked then, only a few years—or months—ago, will not work now. You know why… and you also know what to do about it. You know how to take your business—your line of products and services—to the next level.

You've begun to create your own business model. This is **when** and **where** you start to have something important to write about.

It is also **when** it's valuable to ask yourself, "If I were to write a book, **what** would I want to tell people?"

You: Okay, okay, you win. You're right. I've already started making my list. Let's say this is true.

Me: Good! We're making headway. Now let's say if it is indeed true that you are your best asset, then it is your business to know about yourself. It is also your business to tell others:

- Who you are
- What you represent (your values)
- What your passions are (what you cannot *not* do, in order to be deeply happy)
- Where you want to take your life (your life purpose or mission)
- Your specific goals

Yours and Horton's Who

Most of you probably are familiar with Dr. Seuss' famous story, *Horton Hears a Who.*

Briefly, an imaginative elephant named Horton hears a faint cry for help coming from a tiny speck of dust floating through the air. Although Horton doesn't know it yet, that speck houses an entire city named Who-ville, inhabited by the microscopic Who's, led by the Mayor.

Despite being ridiculed and threatened by his neighbors who think he's lost his mind, Horton is determined to save the particle... because **"a person's a person, no matter how small."**

Horton explains to his skeptical friends: "If you were way out in space and you looked down at where we live, we would look like a speck."

We are all "Horton Who's" living in Whoville. And that's what life is really all about. Each of us is a person and each person is unique.

Whatever you have to say about yourself will include elements that are different from anything anyone has ever written about themselves (or about you).

Regardless of how many books are already out there on business, marketing, entrepreneurship, career building, personal growth, etc.; on line, off line, in the deserts of Arizona or the swamp lands of Florida—coast to coast, shore to shore, around the world in multiple languages—you will NEVER find one that resembles your own or that contains your own personal message expressed just the way only you can express it.

Your book will be written for all those who want to walk in the shoes of uniqueness—their way, not yours—by absorbing everything you have to tell them about "how it's done and why you did it."

Whether you are a plumber, painter, politician, pediatrician, product developer or entrepreneur... no one can replace you. People can tell you that's not true, but deep down you know

without a doubt that you are unique. You have a message to deliver to the world that is different from anyone else's.
Find two snowflakes that are alike. Two pebbles. Two people, even identical twins.

Trust me: your book is going to be different from the one your best buddy writes, or plans to write. Or your cousin Jane. Or your business partner Ted.

Why? Because your experiences are different. Your personalities are different. YOU have something to tell the world about yourself, your mission, your goals and your outlooks that no one else but YOU can express.

And that's why people will want to read your book, work for your company, buy your products and services… or just tell others how lucky they feel because they've had a chance to get to know who you really are.

Which is what your book is all about. You.

Today's 'Who' is never the same as yesterday's

I was thinking of having the subtitle for this book be *Secrets About Yourself That Your Parents Never Could Have Told You.*

Have your parents or some other adult who "knew you when" ever interrupted a conversation with one or more of your business colleagues, or maybe a staff member who has only known you as an adult in your current professional role, with something like:

"I remember when Eric was a baby, he used to pee in the bath water after I had just finished cleaning him up, so I had to start all over again."

Or: "When Susie was five, she was such a rascal. Whenever I took her to the store with me she'd try to steal something—toys or candy, by tucking them under her jacket. One day…"

Your parents might think these stories are cute but you don't, and your colleagues might laugh at them, but, let's face it. They don't have to know about your childhood days, right?

You really *have* come a long way, baby, and sometimes your parents—bless them—might be the last ones who want to admit that.

That doesn't mean you can't add a little fun to your book, such as:

> "He looks like a turnip," Aunt Sally declared when she first peeked at my first photo proudly passed around to family and friends.

How's that for a beginning—something you want to share with the CEO of Major Corporation USA/Germany/ China/Japan? Will that crack them up, make you look like a kook, or will they think you've got some spunk and spark in you because you had the nerve to start your book with a sentence like that?

As they say, you have to know when to hold 'em them and when to fold 'em.

A book you write at this stage in your career—assuming you're not still living under the same roof with your mom and dad—will reveal who you are today. By now you probably know that we are who we become, and that is waaay different from the infant sucking and cooing in the crib—or at least I hope so. It is also not the child you were, growing up and pitching for Little League or playing the violin in the school orchestra.

It is not you as a Boy or Girl Scout, and not you (girl) being photographed in your prom dress or you (boy) behind the wheel of your first car. These are great stories for memoirs, and you might have some interesting episodes to relate that demonstrate what you've learned from the past, or how you were then and how you are now. Other than that, let that You stay photographed and bound in the family album.

At this point in your life you may be president of a company that employs several hundred people and you already have several successes to your credit. Or you may be rapidly climbing the corporate ladder, with many important tips to share with others who are on the same career path.

You are writing this book for all of those people. It is for all of your business associates, colleagues, potential clients and customers, staff, team members, employees, students, and strangers. It is not for your friends and family, unless they want to have an autographed copy for their library: "I knew him or her when."

This book is for people who want to know your values, how you got to where you are today. They want to know your principles — what you stand for. They also want to know about your challenges along the way.

More than anything else, they want to learn from your mistakes, and guess what? You are the only person who can tell them.

They also want to know what makes you tick.... and what makes you different from others. I'm willing to bet that you can deliver on all of these... and more!

3

Why Do I Need a Book?

The naked self

When I went back to school at age 49 to obtain my Masters degree in Creative Writing, I named my thesis, which was a manuscript of poetry, *Naked in Daylight.*

At that time in my life it seemed like a perfect title for a collection of works that exposed who I was, who I was not, and where I wanted to go from there. That time was also a turning point in my life. I was already a traditionally published writer of non-fiction, fiction and poetry. I had served as editor of two literary magazines and had taught business writing, creative writing, English usage, grammar and remedial English at the university level. I'd also taught writing courses in senior centers, rehab centers, and maximum holding/ major felony prisons.

Yet who was I really?

It was time for me to "get naked" not to find out what I wanted to be when I grew up, but to share those hidden aspects of myself that I felt held my greatest value as a human being.

How did I feel about such and such? What did I really think about This or That? Was I truly happy? Why, or why not? In my life thus far, what had caused me the greatest joy? The greatest heartache? Could I describe each of these without being maudlin, getting into the "poor me's" or simply keeping a straight face? I have a raw sense of humor and a caustic tongue. My latest novel, *Slouching Past Bethlehem*, is deliberately raunchy in parts in order to make a point or deliver an important message.

No one wants to read works that are dishonest, that try to cover up the rough spots. We are who we are, warts included.

What are your core values? What do you *really* stand for? What makes your blood curdle, your skin crawl and your hair stand on end? What do you really want to tell people about yourself?

"Getting naked" and exposing who I really was and what I stood for, produced a rich harvest of books and articles. I deliberately titled one of my novels, *The Woman With Qualities*, which is a play on the title of a famous classic, *The Man Without Qualities*, by 20th century Viennese writer, Robert Musil. Like Musil's work, my novel is also about a person searching for their personal value as well as meaning in life. In this instance, however, my work is serious—

based on true events that triggered major changes in my life — whereas Musil's is a satire.

The Real You

I can think of no better way to validate yourself than to go public and introduce The Real You to your potential readers.

In the business world, deception and insincerity don't go very far with staff, customers or colleagues. Qualities of genuineness and sincerity are the foundation for building relationships. Sharing The Real You is also the basis for developing lasting friendships.

A book goes way beyond a handshake or even direct eye contact. It is so much more than the cozy "getting to know you" over a drink or dinner or any other occasion intended for solidifying trust and a comfortable working relationship.

Even the most technical how-to book will deliver the naked truth about the author. They'll tell you where they came from and how they got to where they are today.
Sharing The Real You with your readers is also a way of establishing rapport with them. Most of the Internet gurus who sell how-to and other success-oriented products often use the neat trick of "down dirty sharing" (to the point of *ad nauseum*) in order to establish rapport with potential customers.

Somewhere toward the beginning of their sales page or their books they'll tell you their rags to riches stories. At one time they were homeless and lived on the street... their father or mother was an alcoholic and highly abusive... they grew up on food stamps, or they were dyslexic and in spite of their failing school grades, managed to become a best-selling author, etc.

If you're familiar with the popular DVD *The Secret*, you may have noted that most of the presenters somewhere in the script tell their rags to riches story. They dropped out of school, their dad or mom told them they'd never amount to anything, they had extremely low self-esteem because they were part of an ethnic minority, etc., etc. But guess what? Every one of those "poor me" individuals turned their lives around and rose to the top. Now they're living in multi-million dollar mansions and they have the perfect lifestyle, the perfect partner, etc., etc.

The hidden message is: *if they can do it, so can I.*
Sharing common tears and common fears delivers the bitter-sweet truth that we've all had our ups and downs in one form or other: "...and I want you to know who I really am: where I came from and how far I've come, thanks to my ability to be honest with myself and start to release the stuff that was standing in the way..."

If you have a "get naked" story—and most of us have, your book is the perfect vehicle for delivering it to people with whom you're eager to establish a strong professional or business relationship.

Recently my eldest daughter had to have plastic surgery for the removal of a cyst on her scalp. The situation had gotten out of hand and she was embarrassed about it. She was very hard on herself… why hadn't she taken care of it sooner, etc. The cyst was not malignant, so it wasn't a serious health issue but simply a nuisance. It was a situation that had to be taken care of before it grew larger.

For surgery of this kind, the doctor required several follow-up visits, so she had a chance to meet him in his office, away from the hospital operating room. To her surprise and amazement, she discovered he was not only a human being like herself but he also had a special gift for breaking through the professional veneer and putting his patients at ease. This successful surgeon didn't hesitate to share some very interesting and highly entertaining life stories.

One of the commonalities the two discovered was their love for Vienna. When my daughter was twelve, we lived in Vienna for a year and it was a memorable experience for all of us. Whenever she visited the surgeon's office for a checkup, he would greet her with "Wie geht's?" or "How goes it?" in German. At once they were off talking about their experiences in Vienna while he examined the progress of the (successful) surgery.

The surgeon knew how to establish rapport with his patients, so of course, as a writer, when my daughter related some of his stories, I couldn't help thinking, "This man needs to write a book!"

Business and life are all about relationships

Whether your main "business" in life is about making good profits and getting top results, having a successful personal and social life, experiencing personal satisfaction and inner fulfillment by having done something you're proud of—or all three—it will be about relationships.

That's because the foundation of life itself is relationships. The best novels are rich with colorful, often complex characters interacting with one another. Journalism and other forms of nonfiction include stories about people in relationship with others. Poetry is all about one's personal relationship with people, nature, life's circumstances, God or one's Higher Self.

Every relationship of value is constructed on sincerity, honesty, candor, clear, open communication, and a true desire to share. Your book will also be constructed on those values.

3 - Why Do I Need a Book

You: So now, tell me once again, why it is so important and valuable to share those secrets by writing them down. Tell Me Why...

Me: ...why you should write a book. First of all, it is not about how many copies of your book you're going to sell or how famous your book is going to make you. If that happens, it would be a great bonus. Take it from me: unrealistic expectations or goals that have not been clearly defined—why you're really writing your book—can lead you down a dark alley. A week ago a 65-year-old retired airline pilot and award-winning photographer consulted with me. He'd lost his pension and wanted to recover it by writing a book.

Did he really want to write a book? Well, yes, he said. I asked him what the book would be about. He didn't know. Somehow, somewhere, he'd find something in his life that would be interesting enough to write about *and that would make him a lot of money.*

I wanted to tell him that he should maybe try to win the lottery, or go to Las Vegas and play the slot machines. Getting on all the top talk shows, hitting the *New York Times* best seller list and going over the million mark of copies sold is all part of what can happen, but first you need to have a theme or something you want to say.

If you are an entrepreneur, business owner or professional who is about launch or has already launched their career, you already know what your passion is. Your goal is to tell the world about that passion so your readers will feel as though they already know you when they do business with you, hear you perform a Chopin Polonaise, attend your seminar, call you for consultation, etc.

Think about it. When you create a marketing budget, don't you invest such and such dollars in creating the buzz about your products and services? Why not create buzz about yourself as well, and add the writing and publishing of your book to your marketing budget? Why not start to promote and advertise yourself as part of your company branding?

When you give someone your business card, you don't invoice them (I hope) or hold out your hand and gesture that some shekels need to be dropped into your palm.

Why not consider a book bearing your byline (and contact information at the back) your glorified business card? What better way for potential employees, current staff, customers, clients and the world at large to learn all about you? And of course, you really *can* sell your book, whereas it is just not a good idea to sell your business card.☺

4

The Big How

Years ago, when I first started teaching college writing courses and giving business and creative writing workshops for people of all ages, the first issue that everyone wanted me to address was "writer's block." Surely there must be an easy, fail-safe way to melt that huge chunk of ice in the pit of your stomach that inevitably appears as soon as you sit down at the computer or pick up a pen and wave it over a blank sheet of paper. Blank. The mind goes blank.

Writer's block could also be called the "monkey on the back" syndrome. Someone is judging you and serving as a strict and unforgiveable critic: "You didn't say this right," "you made a grammar mistake there, "this is misspelled…" "how trite this sentence is," etc., etc.

From a psychological perspective, one could say that writer's block is sourced from fear of not getting it right or not being good enough. These are signs of deeply embedded low self-esteem that had its roots in strict teachers, parents or other authoritarian individuals who ruled with an iron hand—or at least you perceived they did. In retrospect, often we realize these teachers may have been merely trying to do their job of injecting your mind with the rules of English grammar and usage.

Sometimes the "not good enough" unconscious implant was the "reward" for writing something so original in your fifth or sixth grade English class, the teacher made fun of it or gave it an F, forcing you to rewrite it. Or maybe one of your teachers told you that you would never be a good writer. Maybe you were the runner-up for a fiction award and from that time on, you told yourself you would never win first place. You would always come in second because you weren't good enough to be first.

However your writer's block happened, I want to reassure you it's easier than you think to dislodge it.

The best and fastest fail-safe way to melt the ice is to **start writing. Anything.** Interesting phrases you overhear. An ad on TV that you can give a twist. A clever idea that pops into your head. The title for a book or a story you might write. A story that someone told you. One of your own stories. You don't even have to read what you write. Just write. And keep writing.

Next: After you've learned those nasty rules, package them up, put a big ribbon around them and store them in the back closet of your mind. Forget about punctuation, grammar, usage—give the monkey a banana and tell him to go outside and play.

Let yourself go.

Here's a helpful exercise:

Pretend you're picking up the phone and your best friend is at the other end. You're telling your friend a hilarious story…

Or you're weeding your garden and chatting to your next-door neighbor, telling them the most interesting tale. Your neighbor is all ears…

The trick is to *just talk.* Be natural. Take out the starch. I never liked starchy anything and I could never figure out why people starched bed sheets and shirt collars unless they enjoyed rashes. Humor intended.

The whole process of living should be fun, and that's one instance when I allow "should" to sneak into my writing. If you can't laugh about it—if you can't be candid and informal—guess what? Nothing will come out!

Push away from the computer and go for a walk or a swim or a run around the block. Loosen up.

Whatever you do and whatever you write: just let it flow. You'll have plenty of time to revise your material. The most important thing right now is to jot it down. Get it into a computer file or on paper. Draft it through and give your monkey another banana. And another. Keep lots of bananas on hand if you have to.

Writing is a Life and Death Matter

Some of you may be familiar with the story of Scheherazade, author of a collection of short stories titled *The Thousand and One Nights*.

Shahryar (Shah-ry-ar), a king in Central Asia, had fallen in love with a beautiful young woman. In Shahryar's kingdom, a woman was property and the king's woman of choice was obliged to be his wife. Case closed.

Unfortunately, this beautiful young woman had a mind of her own and was determined to exercise her right to choose her own partner. Shortly after her marriage to the king, she uh well "transgressed."

When the king learned of her unfaithfulness, he was enraged. We Commoners know what infidelity feels like, but imagine the wrath of a King who believes he is invested with divine power, which includes the right to control other people's minds.

This rebellious young woman was probably tortured to death for her disobedience, and from that time forth, King Shahryar determined he would never allow himself to fall in love with another woman. "Never again will I suffer betrayal!" he vowed.

The king's solution was easy. To protect himself from this painful fate of falling in love, directly after the wedding ceremony, the two would retire to the king's chambers to consummate the marriage and then the king would have his bride murdered.

Needless to say, this agenda did not sit so well with parents who had eligible daughters. Anyone who did the math could see that such a rapid turn-over rate would soon destroy most of the kingdom's beautiful young virgins. What the king wanted, the king could have. Any parent who refused to give their daughter in marriage to Shahyrar was subject to severe punishment. Most likely their fate would be the same as that rebellious young woman who decided no one was going to tell her what to do — not even a king.

Terror reigned in King Shahryar's kingdom until one day a young woman named Scheherazade, concerned for her father's well-being, sent word to the king's vizier that she would consent to marry the king.

Scheherazade was not only beautiful and clever; she was also gifted as a storyteller. Her stories were filled with magic and mystery and they were also pithy. Scheherazade was wise beyond her years.

Even though Scheherazade's father knew about his daughter's storytelling skills (had he not been her teacher?!), he did have a few pangs of discomfort during the wedding ceremony. Nevertheless, he believed in personal sovereignty and what Scheherazade wished, she should have.

On their wedding night, Scheherazade utilized Shahryar's insomnia as an excuse to tell him a story. Come dawn's light, the tale had not yet ended, and the king, eager to know the ending of the story, permitted Scheherazade to live one more night so she could complete it.

Early the next evening, not only did Scheherazade finish telling the first story; she also immediately began telling another... and yet another.

And so it went, for a thousand and one nights. During these almost three years, the king fell deeply in love with this amazing woman and she bore him three children. Shahryar was convinced that never before had a man known such happiness, and to immortalize his lady love, he had Scheherazade's stories, known as *The Thousand and One Nights* written down on scrolls, or, as we say today, published. Today, *The Thousand and One Nights* is considered a classic.

What is the golden nugget or kernel of wisdom that this story conveys? "Love conquers all"—yes, well, of course. And....

NEWS BULLETIN: **Good writing is a life and death matter!**

What's your story?

You'll load your book with stories; anecdotes about your earliest dreams of what you wanted to be when you grew up. Stories about your successes and failures... bloopers, embarrassing moments, times when you really were proud of yourself and times you'd like to forget...This is what people want to read.

They do *not* want a "no show and all tell." Even the starchiest business person doesn't want another handbook or manual. They get enough of these in the workplace.

Your stories will be ***riveting***; chock full of information and details (well-supported), and compelling enough to keep your reader from yawning and heading for the fridge.

The prolific best-selling American author, William Styron, said, "The writer's duty is to keep on writing." I would like to supplement that quote with another: "The writer's duty is to keep the reader turning the page."

Passion - Your passion is the alchemy for generating hot books.

Whatever you write will have sizzle because *you* have sizzle. Never let up on this hi-octane energy.

Personality - Your writing will also have pizzazz... and *it has to be authentically YOU.* Even journalism articles that require objectivity without a trace of opinion or personal commentary, must deliver *your* style or method of delivery. The more you write, the more you will be recognized for your voice or style.

Structure & Organization - Good writing will tease or tantalize at the outset and keep moving toward a goal—delivery of the "take away" or nugget that you wish to deliver. By the time the reader reaches the final page they will be fully satisfied, yet hungering for more (which will be your next book—possibly a business manual or workbook). Can you see how well your personal book fits into your business model?

What goes into the pie?

Jot down all the items you'd like to put into your book: favorite quotations and aphorisms (your commentary about them, preferably relevant to the point you're trying to make or as an embellishment to the story you've just told), important moments in your life, i.e., turning points, moments of decision, descriptions of people who profoundly influenced you and your career, crises that became opportunities, tragedies and how they affected you, high and low points, relevant humorous incidents that demonstrate a certain point, etc.

Keep a notebook by your bedside. Keep another notebook or pad of paper on your desk—on every table in your house, if you have to. Once you start the flow of ideas and let the memories come forth, you'll be amazed how quickly you'll be filling those notebooks. Possibly you'll feel you have enough material for not one but two books... or maybe even three!

Pull out old photo albums or digital files just to bring back relevant memories. Check your digital files for letters and documents, speeches you've written or papers you've given. Interview your relatives. If your parents are still alive, make an appointment with them for a time when you have a chance to be solely alone with them. Not at the barbecue with the grandkids or on the golf course, or while you're watching football. Just the three or two of you over a cup of tea or coffee and your favorite pastries or maybe your mother's famous chocolate chip cookies.

Remember to deliver the visuals and sensuals. Those are the real goods, whether you're writing fiction or non-fiction. Your stories come alive with the tantalizing smell of those fresh home-baked cookies... or the stale, musty cigar-smell of the board room; or the dazzling splendor of the conference room at the Imperial Hotel in Vienna, where you were chosen to head the committee on XXX at the XXX Conference and how it led to XXX...

Deliver the visuals of that moment when the president of the company announced to the Board that you have far exceeded the company's expectations, and he is promoting you to the position of XXX. Describe how you felt at that moment. Or maybe the way your hands trembled when you opened the envelope that confirmed the signed documents for your first big commission to build a skyscraper, design a highway, create an urban historic district, etc.

Tell stories… always more stories, liberally embellished with lots of visuals and sensuals—and always sprinkled with humor. It is said that the ability to laugh at yourself, at your personality quirks as well as your foibles, is the sign of wisdom, maturity, and self-esteem.

Authenticity - Your writing also has to be authentic. This means that you're not posturing or trying to develop the material in order to please a writing professor. You are also not writing with the intention of telling people how much you know or how brilliant you are.

A hungry reader desperate for a genuine experience will not be easily "tricked." Also, anyone who is looking for the real thing will be greatly disappointed to discover a manikin instead of flesh and bone. Plastic surgery and a fake smile don't go very far. Scheherazade was a brilliant young woman who knew how to weave her stories with human insight, compassion and love…

love for humanity and for herself. She was, as they say, the Real Thing. And King Shahryar surely knew that.

Without conceit yet fully self-assured that she had the ability to please the king with her stories, Scheherazade took the ultimate risk and was ready to pay the consequences if necessary.

Focus - You know what you want to say and how you want to say it. This requires a quiet state of relaxed, controlled concentration. You are fully present. When you meet someone and shake their hand or look into their eyes, you can sense if they are sincere.

Likewise, your readers will know from the first lines of your story or article if you are sincerely dedicated to doing your very best to deliver new information or give them a unique and unforgettable reading experience.

Value - The story of Scheherazade delivers another key point: your writing has to have value. If you've ever read *The Thousand and One Nights*, you know each of these stories has human interest or delivers a kernel of wisdom. They are portraits of Scheherazade's inner soul, and it is this beauty, transmitted to King Shahryar at the soul level, that caused him to fall passionately in love with her.

Sustainability – Your readers are your most important commodity, your "King Shahryars"—albeit without the agenda to murder you if you don't deliver a page-turner! You want to nurture these Royal Readers and cultivate a relationship with them so they'll keep coming back for more.

The Big Five

Now that all the ice has melted and the monkeys are off somewhere eating their bananas, you're ready to start writing your book. Write your introduction first. It will probably be completely revised by the time you finish writing the book, but at least it will give you an anchor or starting point as well as a destination. The introduction should include the following:

- ✓ What is this book about?
- ✓ Why did you write it?
- ✓ What is the most important point you want to make—the theme or thread you will carry throughout the book? (This question may overlap with the second one.)
- ✓ What is the take-away for your readers? Again, this may overlap with the theme; it should be related to the theme, but it could be more specific.

If this book is about you and your current business, for example, you may want to define or embellish your business's mission statement, tagline or logo statement. If the theme of the book is larger than just your current business or profession and includes your entire career, you may want to use another quote that has influenced or inspired you through the years.

Remember the man who is a retired surgeon and who now wants to "validate" his life by writing about it? He could choose to use that statement as a theme for his book: "These events were true and because I lived them—created them or was an integral part of them—I feel the need to tell you about them. They will make ME come to life in YOUR eyes."

If you're accustomed to giving speeches or presentations, you already know that one of the great ways to start off is with an anecdote—a humorous story that is original with you, or one that is not often quoted by others. This "warms up" the audience.

Organize your material later

Even if you're the type of person who wants to do things in an orderly manner, when you first set out to write your book, just this once, break out of that pattern.

Remember how you loved to play in the mud or the sandbox and make mud pies? Remember how much you enjoyed finger painting and just "getting into it," whatever it was—without worrying about how dirty you got or whether your hair was getting messed up… Remember the first time you ate ice cream on a stick?

Indulge yourself. Let the ideas come freely and randomly. Let yourself flow and jot down anything that comes into your mind that you feel has value for including in your book. You can organize your material later. Half the fun will be going through all these pieces and patches and stitching them together.

This is one of the best ways to write a book. It is, in fact, the way I've been writing this book and also the way I develop most of my writing.

At any time of the day or night, jot down whatever you feel you'd like to include in your book: thoughts, feelings, stories, beliefs, etc. Our minds are such amazing creatures. If you haven't already discovered it, they even have a mind of their own and come up with the most unusual stories and conversations that they *insist* must be included in your book.

Laundry List

Here are some pointers or things you may wish to include:

- ✓ Mistakes
- ✓ Victories & triumphs – Challenges overcome

- ✓ Bitter-Sweet memories relevant to your theme
- ✓ My teachers
- ✓ Wishes and dreams
- ✓ Current problems or challenges
- ✓ Advice for beginners
- ✓ Advice for intermediates
- ✓ What would you have done differently if you had a chance to do it again?
- ✓ My company (profession, career, etc.)
  - ○ What makes it or me unique?
  - ○ What's my style?
- ✓ My hobbies
- ✓ My family
- ✓ My biggest supporters

5

Should I Contract a Ghostwriter or Book Doctor?

Life in the fast track becomes a lot simpler when you take advantage of professional resources. When it comes to working with a ghostwriter, book doctor or editor, these services are now available worldwide, thanks to the Internet. My own client base is global, and this is easily managed through Internet services such a skype for free computer-to-computer audio- and video-calling and recording. Webcam is another excellent feature, in addition to instant messaging and emailing.

For projects that involve a book that needs to be written "from scratch," especially autobiographies and works that contain proprietary information, I request a face-to-face meeting with my clients shortly after we've signed the contract. This personal meeting on an energetic level is invaluable. It gives me a chance to experience the style of that person and how they want me to represent them in their book.

I spend a minimum of four full days with a new client, interviewing and recording their story. Added to this will be their written materials, e.g., lectures, articles, news clips, etc.

Book doctoring, unless it requires a total overhaul of a manuscript, including additional input from the client, does not require a personal meeting. Editing, whether advanced (requiring a small amount of manuscript re-organization and restructuring, or normal line editing)—also does not require a personal meeting. Certainly if desired, webcam is available.

Below is a copy of the document I send out to potential clients who are seeking a ghostwriter:

5 - Should I Contract a Ghostwriter or Book Doctor?

What Does a Ghostwriter Do?

Following are the steps I take with my client after I sign a contract with them:

- Set up a time to meet with them vis-à-vis to spend 4-5 full working days recording all the material for the book.

- Request all the supportive documents, written material, graphics and other resource items that the client may wish to include in the book; these can be given to me during my visit or they can mail them to me shortly thereafter.

- Upon returning from my visit with the client, I transcribe the recorded sessions and start to organize the material into categories.

- At the same time, I organize the supplemental material into categories that can be integrated with the transcribed material.

- At that point, I can visualize the structure of the book.

- I set to work organizing the book chapters or divisions.

- I then "weave" together all of the material by moving through it categorically; sorting, discarding, making notes about areas where I need more input from the client, etc.

- I proceed to develop the first 50 pages of the book, which I send to the client for their input.

- I make the necessary adjustments and then proceed to develop the first draft of the entire work.

- Upon completion (it will have been proofed several times already), I send that draft to the client.

- The client reviews it carefully and then we work together to make the revisions. During this stage, often the client needs tutoring. I work closely with them, adjusting my schedule to fit their needs and often demonstrating how to effectively make these revisions.

Do You Really Need To Write A Book?

- The client starts to send back the revised material, either a chapter at a time, or in larger segments.

- I make all of the necessary adjustments and then return the completed second draft to the client.

- The client reviews the second draft and makes other adjustments and editorial changes.

- After receiving the second draft, I make these adjustments, carefully proofread the finished manuscript several times and make the necessary corrections, then send it to the client. At this point it is considered a finished work.

- If the client wishes to make additional adjustments, I charge an hourly rate until we have satisfactorily completed the process.

- The manuscript is now ready to be published.

My clients have the option of co-publishing with Dandelion Books, my company, or they can submit their work to a traditional publisher. Sometimes they choose a third option of opening their own publishing company.

My goal when working with a client is to deliver a product that:

1. aligns with their energy, intent and message
2. delivers a fresh, original approach to the subject matter, if it is a non-fiction work
3. is highly creative and compelling, if it is a fiction work
4. reads well
5. is as free as possible from grammatical errors, "glitches" and typos, i.e., is ready to publish, with a suggested 2-3 more proof reading run-throughs by at least one pair of eyes different from the client's and the ghostwriter's

Concerning No. 5, additional proofreading, it is a well-known fact that after working intensively on a manuscript, the author no longer "see" the errors because their eyes have accepted them. I like to set aside a large manuscript for at least a week to ten days before proofing it once again. (By the time I deliver a completed work to a client, I have edited and proofed it at least eight full times through, for each process.)

Guilt-Free Ghostwriting

Many people feel it isn't fair to have someone else write their book. They have a sense of guilt because they feel they should be doing the work themselves.

Let me reassure you that most super-busy people in this world do not write their own articles, speeches and books; we can now add blogs and other social networking items to that list. They have a large staff to perform this type of work. Remember the person at the beginning of this book who complained they didn't even have time to brush their teeth?

Time is our most valuable commodity. It is a rare person who has learned how to use time wisely and also to catch the rhythm of work and play without feeling guilty either about "taking time off" or having to work overtime at the office and miss a family or social event.

At some point in their lives, every competent professional learns how to delegate and duplicate or replicate. I'm preaching to the choir as I write this because I confess, I have so much fun writing, it doesn't ever seem to fit into the category of "work." Most of the time it feels more like play.

Yet it is a fact that even those of us who are passionate about our work need time for rest and rejuvenation. We need time to be with the family, intimate time with one's significant other, time to travel—all of these are an integral part of a lifestyle that is healthy, wholesome and constructive.

For those of you who are honest with yourselves and can admit without guilt that getting a book written doesn't seem like something you'll *ever* find time to do, a ghostwriter is a perfect solution. Or, if you've never had a desire to write a book or write anything, for that matter—if you are more of a vocal or aural person, you will welcome the opportunity to have a ghostwriter help you get it down on paper.

I have several friends and colleagues who are great speakers and seminar leaders. Just put them in front of the microphone and let them take off! They're spellbinding. Give them a computer keyboard or a pen and piece of paper and they fall apart. *Vive le difference!*

Then there are those who are excellent at the keyboard, but watch out for all the spelling and usage errors! I like to work with these people because usually they have creative minds that are chock full of ideas and they're whizzing all over the place in several dimensions all at once. Rather than try to tame them, I like to simply let them talk and then organize the material later, when I'm alone with a cup of chamomile tea ☺

The usage and grammar skills they lack are secondary to their creative mind and where it takes them. I enjoy the challenge of working with highly gifted individuals who have this type of talent.

The other day three women who wrote a book asked me to develop a test sample of how I would line edit it. They confessed that none of them had writing skills beyond jotting down their stories. The job would require both a skillful and creative line editor, they informed me, and the test they gave me included a demonstration of both.

Here is the response I received from the woman who was in charge of running the test:

> On Thu, Oct 15, 2009 at 12:45 PM, Axxxx <Axxxx@_____> wrote:
>
> Oh WOW! I can't even begin to express my utter excitement! You exceeded my expectations for sure. You did an amazing job with just so little information and yet you know exactly what we were meaning to say or what we would have said. And you nailed it...I totally had envisioned my life in a downtown loft overlooking the city. A's section you did so well, it has her witty and fabulous attitude, and M...you could not have done a better re-write on that. I just forwarded it to the girls so they can read it and be just as excited as me!
>
> I will be in touch soon.
>
> Axxxx

I've copied this email not because I need to blow my own horn or tell people how good I am, but rather, to reinforce the belief that

EVERY qualified, experienced ghost writer, book doctor and line editor should be able to complete similar tests and get the same type of response.

Obviously I don't have samples of the other tests that were submitted to these three women, so I don't know how their work compared to mine, but I can only tell you that for me, it was not a difficult challenge; it was in fact, one that I thoroughly enjoyed.

If you don't really enjoy what you do, if it seems laborious—stop! Find another profession!

Mutual trust, clarity and understanding

My goal is always to establish a strong, trusting relationship with my clients. Included in that trust is reassurance that I will do my best to deliver a product that meets their expectations and that also has top market value. I work together with each client until I've developed a manuscript that satisfies all requirements for both of us. This involves clarity, mutual understanding, desire "to do what it takes" without the clock running, and a professional attitude. This means one must be willing to give the client the benefit of the doubt—they do know what they want—and guide them toward decisions that will be aligned with their goals.

I work with manuscripts in all stages of development. Sometimes a client has already drafted the work and needs help revising it.

Often part of the work is written, the client gets stuck and calls for help. Or sometimes the work simply needs a good line editor.

I also write book proposals

Often when a person decides not to self-publish and wishes to find a traditional publisher via a literary agent, I'll write the book proposal, which includes the following:

- Cover letter
- Pitch Document (2-3 pages)
- Table of Contents
- Chapter Summaries
- Synopsis
- Sample Chapters
- Author's Bio
- Marketing & Promotion Plan
- Competition Analysis

Initial conferences by phone or in person are free. (Sometimes a potential client either lives in the area or will travel to meet with me). All services are included in my flat rate fee with the exception of travel expenses when interviews are necessary or research is involved.

I feel fortunate and grateful to have worked with so many extraordinary individuals; I am a willing student of my clients. I learn so much from them, so I always feel the rewards of my work are at least twofold.

> In ordinary life we hardly realize that we receive a great deal more than we give, and that it is only with gratitude that life becomes rich.
> —Dietrich Bonhoeffer

6

Publishing & Promoting Your Book

"For better or for worse," the knot has now been tied between The Elite and The Masses in the world of publishing. Also "for better or for worse," this is a marriage that is bound, or doomed to last.

At the 2009 60th annual National Book Awards ceremony, host and comedian Andy Borowitz said when he was first invited to emcee the awards, he was so honored, he told them that he'd have done it for free. As it turned out, he quipped, "The NBA (National Book Association) had the same idea." And when it comes to the economics of the publishing world, Borowitz said, "We're all in the same sinking ship."
http://features.csmonitor.com/books/2009/11/19/2009-national-book-award-winners/

Burnham Woods has come to Dunsinane *—and none too soon as far as the growing group of outstanding authors (The Masses) is concerned. Bleeding from multiple stabs of undeserved pink rejection slips, they now realize that for too long they've been slighted by an industry that was never set up to publish hundreds of thousands of books annually. It was never even set up to publish one hundredth of the outstanding books that deserve to be out there in the marketplace.

Bottom Line: Today, just as in the automobile industry, the resulting hybrids of **traditional, co- and self-publishing companies** often operating under the same corporate roof **are here to stay**, often not by choice but by necessity. The masses, aka savvy online authors and marketers, are already eating cake.** The Internet has been a boon to entrepreneurs and marketing gurus—*especially for those who understand the value of using a book with their byline as a marketing tool.*

Digital technologies came, saw and conquered the marketplace and this is a fact that no traditional publisher can ignore. That they have "evolutionized" the publishing industry is another fact that Wall Street as well as the corporate media moguls have been forced to accept—even though at times the truth has been hard going down. Collapse of the print newspaper and magazine industries are imminent and no one can deny that the latest business model for the book industry—1) print on demand hard copy books, 2) virtual books delivered wirelessly or as downloads to computers and reading devices, and 3) books instantly printed at the point of sale—are both a reader's and writer's bonanza. For the entrepreneur and business owner, a book bearing their byline is even more than that because of the value it adds to their promotional toolkits.

The Information Age and advent of the Internet with the World Wide Web followed by sophisticated search engine technologies have turned book-buying strategies upside-down. Instead of publishers dictating what readers should buy, readers are telling publishers what they need to produce—and if they refuse, all is not lost. They'll publish the works themselves.

For the enterprising business person who knows how to brand and create trends, a book reinforces the link between you and your customers or the public at large. It sets the tone of trust, quality and dependability that gives people that feeling of doing business with someone you feel you know personally even if you don't.

Never before has the world been friendlier to book authors and never before have there been so many venues for publishing and selling books.

A brief history of publishing

Not so long ago, unless you wanted to be labeled a "vanity author," your works had to be published by a traditional publisher. "Vanity" was a term that was frowned upon by elitist publishers, published authors and any writer who took their career seriously.

They never would have *considered* vanity or self-publishing. Today that term has taken its place among hoop skirts, corsets and button-hook elbow length gloves. It is not only archaic and outmoded but has also undergone a serious semantic face lift. "Vanity" publishing is now known as "self-publishing" and in most business sectors is treated with the utmost respect because of its marketing and advertising potential.

Traditional publishing and how it works

A writer submits their finished manuscript either directly to a publisher or in more recent times, indirectly through a literary agent. Today most of the large traditional publishers will not accept unsolicited manuscripts. The literary agent shops your book to appropriate publishers or to the ones with whom they have "connections." Politics has always played a key role in getting a book on the desk of the editor-in-chief. We need to be honest about that, just as we need to be honest about "vanity" publishing in former days.

Often, unless they looked for the evidence, the reading public never learned that a significant percentage of traditionally published books were subsidized by a private foundation, benefactor or corporation. Subsidies were in the form of grants and charitable donations from foundations or trusts, or they were simply business arrangements made between the CEO and marketing director of a large corporation and the publisher.

An agreement to buy the first print run of 10,000 books within the first 30 days at retail price creates a best seller. Or, simply the sponsorship of a print run of over 10,000 copies gives the publisher enough capital to produce the book and get it into distribution.

A traditional publisher pays all the production and administrative expenses. They used to make the full investment in marketing and promotion as well, but today, unless the author is well-known, this is no longer part of the package. In fact, often the publisher requires a commitment from the author to deliver a certain sum to be applied toward the "marketing budget."

They may also request a new author to contract a publicist for at least six months to a year after the book reaches the street. These are things the author learns about after the book has been accepted and they're about to sign on the dotted line. At that point they may be so excited to be working with a bona fide "traditional publisher," they'll spend two or three times the amount on a publicist than they would have spent had they self- or co-published their book. (Remember, no publisher can guarantee sales, especially for a new or unknown author. Therefore, in a marketplace glutted with new books, whether a new or unknown author publishes traditionally or self-publishes, the stakes are almost the same.)

The author retains the copyright for the book; a publisher merely acquires a license to publish and sell it. The author will receive a royalty or percentage of the sale price of each book sold. ("Sale price" can be significantly different from the "list price." Amazon.com, for example, discounts most books.)

Books that are traditionally published have certain advantages over self- or co-published books:

- Media will interview the author (especially if the publisher and media network are owned by the same corporation).
- Top of the line literary magazines and publishing trade journals, including library journals (the ones that give the nod to acquisition directors and bookstore buyers) will review the books.
- Brick & mortar bookstores will give the book shelf space (at least for 30 days; if the book catches on, shelf and display space and time will be extended).
- Brick & mortar bookstores will also welcome book signings, readings and appearances. They may even invest in marketing and advertising (especially if the stores are partly owned by the publishing /media conglomerate).

It would seem that an author should be thrilled to have their manuscript accepted by a traditional publisher because: 1) they don't have to pay any of the production costs and may not have to pay marketing and promotion costs, although this is becoming rare, and 2) they get the best possible media coverage, free.

The cold hard truth

Most books don't make it past the 30-day point and the game is over almost before it begins. Books that don't catch fire and start to deliver significant sales numbers will be removed from brick & mortar bookshelves and trucked back to the distributors' and wholesalers' warehouses where they will be inventoried to collect dust (and fees paid by the publisher) until sold off as remainders, returned to the publisher at the publisher's expense, or destroyed.

Publishing would be a losing business if not for a few staple categories, such as diet books, cookbooks, chick lit, romance and whodunits; and the publisher's stall of celebrity authors. Publishers owned by film companies can also make up for losses through subsidiary rights or other versions of the book as films, DVDs, etc.

Timing is everything

If a literary agent accepts your manuscript, they will then shop the book to all the appropriate traditional publishers in order to obtain the best advance against royalties. This sum of money is a built-in guarantee that the author will receive some type of compensation up front before books are sold, since usually it takes at least six to nine months before the book hits the street or can be purchased in retail bookstores.

In today's fast-paced digital age, all of these procedures are not only old-fashioned; usually they are also undesirable. Information that is current when the book is accepted for publication can be outdated by the time the book becomes available. With the right contacts and financial backing, however, the publishing process can be hastened.

Every savvy business person involved in one way or other in the book industry is well aware of what it takes in to order to make the best sellers' lists and stay there for more than a week. It's very exciting when it happens and I celebrate all those who choose to seek a literary agent and traditional publisher. I also celebrate their patience and perseverance.

I hope I haven't repeated this too many times: If a traditional publisher asks you, the author, to pay for most of the marketing and promotion, it no longer makes any difference WHO the publisher is. If you don't do a good job and the book fails to produce significant sales numbers, the publisher will shrug their shoulders, say "too bad," and move on.

This is not an uncommon experience. Authors have come to me with this sad sack story because usually they and not the publisher are the ones who take the loss. The small advance

6 - Publishing & Promoting Your Book

against royalties and sometimes only a net instead of a gross percentage of the sales (a word to the wise: NEVER sign a net publishing contract!) will hardly deliver their return on investment for the required (ambitious) marketing and promotion budget.

Some authors report an advantage to having their books on the shelves of brick & mortar stores. As I stated previously, this means they or their publicist can do book signings and speaking engagements in these establishments.

This opportunity is not available to authors who use the digital print on demand method of publishing, because bookstores do not stock and will not sell digitally printed, i.e., print on demand books except possibly on consignment. There's a reason for this.

If you publish your books on demand, you cannot use—or rather you would prefer not to use—a distributor or wholesaler (the procedure used by traditional publishers).

Distributors and wholesalers ask for 60% of the retail price of every book sold through their warehousing and "schlepping" procedure that ultimately lands the books in the retail brick & mortar stores.

When you do the math, since the unit cost of a print on demand book is so much higher than the unit cost of an offset printed book that is part of a large print run, a large chunk of the profits for intermediaries such as distributors and wholesalers is simply not possible. Very little is left for the publisher and author; often the net is a figure in the red.

Bottom line: Digital print on demand does not work for indirect distribution. The two systems are diametrically opposed. Digital on demand printing was made for online direct marketing and sales. It is a perfect match, since no intermediaries are necessary.

Realistically, most authors report that brick & mortar bookstore book signings usually do not net more than the sale of a handful of books, unless one is a celebrity author and the signing is attended by hundreds of fans rather than twenty or thirty friends.

Another reality check: Even the most lavish budget for TV infomercials and ads will not do the job *if you cannot deliver.* In addition to being a competent writer, you must also be an expert promoter and public speaker. If you are charismatic, you've won half the battle. The other half must be won through innovative marketing and advertising techniques. Every publisher will be honest about this. They'll tell you they can produce a quality product, and if they are a New York publisher they can get you in the door for the right media interviews, TV and radio talk shows, etc., but ultimately **you the author will have to do the rest.** (Have I repeated this too many times?!)

6 - Publishing & Promoting Your Book

There's no such thing as a prima donna today who can simply say to the publisher: "Do me. Make me famous." It's just won't happen. In the past, it did happen in a few instances when a first-rate editor at a traditional publishing house took an interest in a new writer and book doctored their works. And it did happen in the case of Harry Potter. Scholastic Books took an interest in JK Rawlings' first book and signed a contract with her. From that point on, the works became the product of the combined skills of the Scholastic Books editorial board, bearing the author's byline. Scholastic Books made JK Rawlings famous. It was good business to do so. They've made a fortune, or a "killing," as they say. Such success stories are rare.

Self and Co-Publishing

Today self-publishing and co-publishing are the most popular ways to get your works published. Not only is it less expensive than in the past, since print runs are now no longer necessary (the preferable model is print on demand or short low-cost digital print runs); but also, if you know how to maneuver on the Internet, *you can create your own book marketing empire.*

Competition among the few remaining traditional publishers who have not gone bankrupt or been sold off to a large corporate operation is so keen, few people choose to play the literary agent roulette game for months and sometimes years before a possible contract arrives.

> If we are our most important assets, time is our most valuable commodity. Save time, money and energy: invest in yourself. You're worth it, and so is your book.

As I put the finishing touches on this manuscript, Google is working on a master plan to sell hundreds of thousands of books through its search engine operations. In competition with Amazon.com's Kindle book reader and Apple Book applications, this is bound to be a race without a finish line. Amazon Kindle (www.amazon.com) has just made all of its titles available for downloading directly onto a PC. Downloading software is free. Barnes & Noble online (www.bn.com) also has its own free downloading software for ebook purchase.

Contrary to what some industry analysts are predicting, I believe that instead of destroying the hard copy book industry, ebook publishing will serve as an enhancement. The Espresso Book Machine® makes it easy and low cost to print books within a few minutes at the place of sale.

States the Ondemandbooks.com website:

> What Gutenberg's press did for Europe in the 15th century, digitization and the Espresso Book Machine® will do for the world tomorrow.
>
> Library quality paperbacks at low cost, identical to factory made books, printed direct from digital files for the reader in minutes,

> serving a radically decentralized world-wide multilingual marketplace.
>
> *Espresso*: something made to order, one at a time, at point of sale, quickly.

Ebooks are simply another bonus for modern authors—a great one.

Today a book should be published simultaneously in:

- Hard copy version, i.e., designed and laid out by a professional or someone who is extremely experienced in using one of the book publishing programs (InDesign or Quark Xpress, for example); two files, front & back cover, and spine; and the interior or contents, that is converted to a pdf file.

- Ebook versions
    - The same file for the interior of the hard copy book, with a different ISBN number*** and a 3-D cover.
    - An Amazon Kindle digitally converted file (rich text format of MS Word), and a 2-D cover based on Kindle specifications
    - Mobile conversions (xxl, etc.) for smart phones; no cover necessary

Through Lighting Source International, you can also make your books available in hard copy for instant print-out on the Espresso

Book Machine®. Espresso Book Machines® are already located in several prominent places throughout the world, and more are on the way.

For business persons, entrepreneurs and anyone on the career track, however, as I mentioned previously, yet another distribution venue is now open that delivers 1) the best profits, 2) sales and marketing leads, and 3) a loyal following.

That option is **your own website and your own web business.** If you're fortunate to have a large staff that is already computer and Internet savvy—and no doubt they are—you can create a launching pad specifically for your book.

Here's the plan:

1. For each book you publish, create a website or blog that is either free-standing or connects to your other websites and blogs.
2. When you build your web pages, focus on SEO and keyword identification for the search engines.
3. Start to social network through multiple venues (Facebook, MySpace, Twitter, LinkedIn, Xing, Ning, and all the focused special interest groups pertaining to your business or enterprise).
4. Create a squeeze page or sales page. Include testimonials and endorsements. You may wish to create a Joint Venture

6 - Publishing & Promoting Your Book

with individuals who provide endorsements so you can pool opt-in email lists.

Previously I mentioned giving your book away and I pointed out that often this idea is greeted by shock until or unless a savvy business person perceives it as an investment.

I'm sure you know how many millions of dollars are spent on media ads. Why not consider your book an advertisement for you and your business?

This is the best way to view any publishing venture. I'm quick to point out to anyone who comes to me for co-publishing with my company, Dandelion Books (www.dandelion-books.com) that 1) they, the author, are in charge of marketing and promotion—I can put them in touch with excellent offline and online marketing and promotion people, but Dandelion is only the publisher; 2) it is extremely important not to ask how many books one needs to sell in order to break even on one's investment. To release that thought process which often becomes an obsession and ultimately turns into a failure model, I suggest that the book be categorized as a marketing and promotion tool rather than a stand-alone product. Whatever profits are generated from sales can be re-invested in advertising and promotion.

Note how this strategy changes the whole perspective of exactly *what this book is* and *how it is to be used*. The truth is: authors who write quality books will only begin to understand the value of their product after they've published it and start to get feedback from their readers. It's simply a matter of being in the flow of abundance and understanding how the marketplace works.

We're living in a digital, electronic multi-media age

If you choose to work with a co-publishing company, i.e., a company that you contract to do all the production and print setup, you will want to work with one that understands and uses "on demand" printing and distribution.

If you're considering placing your book with a publisher that does not have a website, use the Internet or any other digital technologies—beware! This is a sign that they would have a difficult time completing pre-press and post-press book production processes efficiently and economically.

Today's online book marketing and promotion capabilities far surpass any type of exposure and publicity that currently exists through other venues, especially for new or unknown authors. It's another red flag if a publisher is unfamiliar with Web 2.0 marketing technologies and if viral marketing and social networking are not part of their promotion package.

More about Print on Demand (POD)

In the book industry, on-demand usually refers to "print on demand" and is abbreviated as "POD." It is now becoming SOP (standard operating procedure) to print books at the time of purchase, after the customer has paid for them.

At the turn of the century, POD took the book industry by storm and by 2004 it had gained such a stronghold, the handwriting was "virtually on the wall": Gutenberg & Co.—most forms of offset printing using metal plates and rollers—were on their way to the graveyard. Today a small table-top printer (The Espresso Book Making Machine®) can produce "15-20 library quality paperback books per hour" –a process that only a few years ago used to take days.

If Gutenberg led to literacy, POD has led to poderacy. Taken to the ultimate, POD dispensed with the need to:

- Warehouse books and pay all the warehousing fees, insurance, taxes, etc., etc. As soon as a book is purchased, it is printed from files archived in the digital printing equipment. Within 48 business hours, it's on its way to the customer.
- Pay huge sums of money to an offset printer for large print runs.

- Use wholesalers and distributors for trucking cartons from wholesaler to distributor to bookstore warehouses, and finally to the bookstore, where the customer purchases an often war-torn looking product.
- Force the publisher to take the loss of returned and often damaged books.
- Invest huge sums of money to print a second edition if the author wishes to correct errors or make other editorial changes… and suffer the loss of an out-dated first edition.

Today, most publishers use digital printing unless a book requires a large print run. Recently, Lightning Source International introduced speedy offset printing for larger print orders. Printing companies can now use digitally implemented "hybrid" models that are more efficient and economical for any size print run.

Obviously, anything manufactured in volume will be more cost effective than one-off or on demand production. Also, if a book requires special high resolution reproductive work that a digital printer may be incapable of performing, it will be offset printed. As digital printers continue to become more sophisticated, however, this will no longer be a challenge.

Welcome to the 21st century where you, the author, are in charge of your publishing options and the finished product.

More about the Espresso Book Making Machine® and the Backlist

Book printing has taken a giant leap forward not only off the page and virtually "into space," but also reincarnating in digital format through an amazing device known as the Espresso Book Making Machine.®

Jason Epstein, former editorial director of Random House and founder and CEO of On Demand Books, the company that markets the Espresso, is one of the pioneers of the new book printing and storage revolution.

The backlist—backbone of the book industry

In 1951 when Epstein went to work for Doubleday, it didn't take long for him to learn that the key to book industry survival is "backlist."

As Epstein expounded in his 2008 Hong Kong Book Fair address, publishing cannot exist without backlist:

"Backlist is a publisher's most important asset: titles that have covered their initial costs, earned out the authors' advances, require no further investment except the cost of making and shipping the book itself and which sell steadily year after year without advertising or significant sales expense."

"Without a substantial list of such titles a publisher cannot survive," stated Epstein. "The same can be said of a civilization, for the books that survive the test of time, books that are treasured and read year after year, are humanity's backlist, our collective brain.

"I do not refer simply to the classics of our various traditions but also to the more recent books," continued Epstein, "hundreds of which are published every year and join the backlist if not permanently at least long enough to move the process forward, providing depth and complexity to our understanding for those who seek it.

"Backlist deepens our knowledge of human experience past and present. Without these books we would not know who we are or where we came from or where we may be going."

Publishers are secular priests

"Publishing is not really a business at all, at least not a very good business," declared Epstein. "If it's money you want to make, go into a real business and take your chances… publishing is a vocation, a secular priesthood for publishers are caretakers of our collective memory, indispensable servants to those other caretakers, poets, story tellers, librarians, teachers and scholars."

Did I cringe when I read that statement? I hope so—otherwise I, like many other publishers would be living in denial. Every serious publisher is well aware that it's not the brass ring of a best seller but something else far more significant that motivates us to dedicate ourselves to delivering quality books.

We "secular priests" are also deeply committed to the backlist: preservation of the written word. If only one person finds value in a book that is out of print, it is worth the effort to re-issue that work and make it available.

Epstein's backlist mission began with the creation of paperback books, which cost less and were also easier on the publishers' budget. However, paperbacks still required print runs that often led to out of print books and investments in inventory and warehousing.

Print on Demand – Backlist Bonanza

The major breakthrough occurred when digital technologies burst into the marketplace and print on demand became a reality.

As a writer who signed a contract with one of the major publishers for a book that was censored shortly after it appeared, and as a publisher who opened one of the first "traditional" online publishing companies in 2000, I knew we were on the brink of a book industry revolution. I realized that the digital on demand production and delivery technologies were a way to save the backlist... *and* also distribute censored books to a public hungry for the truth. The Internet was a refreshingly free and open venue where it seemed possible to avoid censorship and book banning—at least for awhile.

"Books written last year, ten years or a hundred years ago will always be available, thanks to print on demand," I wrote in newsletters and press releases that described the Dandelion vision.

I recalled looking forward to a time when we would be able to provide one-off book buying and seamless order and fulfillment from a shopping cart website.

Colleagues thought I was crazy. "It'll never happen," they retorted.

"And then," I added, ignoring their rebuttals, "one day someone will come up with a portable print on demand machine that will print books a minute at a time. Like a jukebox, the buyer will punch in the letter and number code, press the 'Start' button and out of the chute will slide a perfectly produced paperback book. We can then place these glorified printers in bookstores, coffee houses, libraries... wherever people want to read, discuss and buy books."

"It'll never happen," my colleagues repeated.

Today, thanks to Jason Epstein's Espresso Book Making Machine® and his mission to save the backlist, it *has* happened... and all the nay-sayers are now jumping on the bandwagon.

Do your research

Once your manuscript is finished and ready to go into production, do your homework before deciding how you want to publish it.

In the checklist below I've separated book and article publishing, since you may wish to do both. I certainly encourage publishing articles as well as full-length manuscripts, especially if they'll give you good name exposure that could help promote your book as well as your company.

Books

- ✓ Study the book industry. Learn everything there is to know about publishing.
- ✓ Research industries related to book publishing (audio books, ebooks, films, etc.).
- ✓ Visit many publishing websites.
- ✓ Become familiar with book industry associations (Literary Marketplace, Publishers Marketing Association, etc.).
- ✓ Join writing and publishing forums.

- ✓ Learn how to write a book proposal.
- ✓ Learn how to develop a media kit.
- ✓ Interview authors to learn how they publish.
- ✓ Interview literary agents.
- ✓ Interview publishers and editors.
- ✓ Be sure to check out my website at http://www.write-to-publish-for-profit.com –all the links, including blog articles.
- ✓ Feel free to contact me with your questions and concerns.

Articles

- ✓ Submit your articles wherever the guidelines fit your work.
- ✓ Add the titles of your published pieces to your résumé.
- ✓ Post articles freely on appropriate websites.
- ✓ Volunteer to be a regular web columnist.
- ✓ Start a blog.
- ✓ Podcast and post.
- ✓ Collect your articles and publish them as a book.
- ✓ Stay current with free lance writing classifieds.
- ✓ Develop a fee structure sheet; send it when requested.
- ✓ Write for off-line media whenever possible.
- ✓ Learn how to write publicity, advertising and marketing copy.

6 - Publishing & Promoting Your Book

✓ Feel free to contact me with your questions and concerns.

*In Shakespeare's famous tragedy, *Macbeth,* Macbeth goes to the witches' den, where a naked coven shows him a vision of a threatening Macduff and then assures him that "none of woman born shall harm" him. They tell him he will survive until "the Burnham Wood comes to Dunsinane (name of Macbeths' castle)." Alas, eventually the "forest" does indeed come to Dunsinane in the form of soldiers decked with tree branches from Burnham Wood. "The jig is up." Macbeth's crime of killing the King (Duncan) is exposed.

**"Let them eat cake" is the traditional translation of the French phrase *"qu'ils mangent de la brioche,"* supposedly said by a French princess upon learning that the peasants had no bread. The quotation, as attributed to Marie Antoinette, was claimed to have been shouted during one of the famines that occurred in France during the reign of her husband, Louis XVI (1754-1793).

*** ISBN - International Standard Book Number (ISBN) is a unique numeric commercial book identifier used by booksellers. Every version of a book has a different ISBN number. Publishers buy them in blocks from R. R Bowker and assign a number to each title. The ISBN number appears on the copyright page. A book is also registered with the U.S. Copyright Office and Library of Congress through its ISBN number as well as its title, author and publisher. The ISBN prefix of numbers serves as an identifier to the publisher.

7

Bottom Line

Now that I've touched on the basics for writing and publishing your book, I want to give you more of my personal opinions about writing, writers, publishing and the book industry in general.

What I believe in

> ❖ Quality content
> ❖ Quality writing
> ❖ Quality publishing

Notice how many times I've repeated the word *quality.* I stand behind quality work and quality service. I give my all to my clients and I want them to know that. I am deeply committed to delivering a product that looks good and reads well. If my clients aren't satisfied with the drafted material I've completed for them, I reassure them we'll start over. I'll be there for them until we get it right!

The same standards hold true for my publishing business. We are a boutique co-publishing company, which means that unlike most online turnkey web businesses that produce whatever is submitted and call it a book, we accept only a small percentage of the manuscripts that are submitted to us.

I or a competent member of my staff personally read a portion of every manuscript. Usually I can tell within the first 20-25 pages whether the author is on target with their material, has something valuable to say and is saying it in a unique way. I do not intend to be dismissive, but after awhile, it becomes obvious if a work is not yet ready to be published. Some writers may submit a work that has potential but may still need a great deal of work. Often, however, they are unwilling to admit this ("my word is the word of God... don't you dare change one word, etc.").

If I feel a work isn't ready for publishing but the author feels otherwise—if they really want to get a book out there, I suggest they go to one of the many turnkey online companies to publish it. Rates are reasonable and some don't charge anything at all. I don't know who's paying the salaries of their book designers, editors and proofreaders, but if their business model works for them and they're making profits, all the more power to them.

I do know, however, that I wouldn't entrust my work to an online self-publishing company that promises free editing and proofreading.

If you shop around, you'll find a variety of co-publishing and publishing service packages as well as self-publishing ones. I offer consulting services for those who are confused about the different packages or about the wording of a publishing contract.

Recently I served as a publishing consultant for a man who was about to sign with a co-publishing company that offered an interesting contract. They did not charge for editing, proofreading, book cover and interior design and layout. Their only fee was for the purchase of 500 books—at print cost.

They also offered wholesaling and distribution. This meant the books could be sold not only online but also through brick & mortar bookstores. To fulfill the brick & mortar bookstore requirement, as I mentioned earlier, this meant the books would have to be printed offset rather than digitally. (It is an industry requirement that only books that are printed offset are entitled to be placed in brick & mortar bookstores.)

This publishing company also offered free marketing and promotion services.

I was amazed because it seemed to be the best of all possible worlds and yet I couldn't understand how they could make any money. The book in consideration was 600 pages—twice the size of a standard book these days. Most digital or online publishers would suggest that it be divided in two or cut down to approximately 300 pages. The reason for this is the simple mathematics of digital printing. The unit cost for a print on demand book always stays the same, regardless of how many books one prints—unless one prints over 3000 books at a time. The unit cost will then start to drop. However at that point, often the book will be printed offset—a longer process without the benefits of digital printing—because the unit cost will be even less.

A book that is 600 pages in length would have a very high print cost because the unit cost is based on the total number of pages. In order to make significant profits, the publisher must charge *at least* three times the print cost, to allow for retailer discounts (online bookstores usually discount the list price). The high retail cost would influence sales significantly.

Many editors candidly state, "If you can't say it in 300 pages, it's not worth saying." In other words, it is critically important to learn how to be succinct. Readers are turned off by books that become repetitive and boring. Most often, unless the book requires extensive footnotes, quoted material, diagrams, photos and graphics, I've discovered it could easily be given a good barbering.

Added to all of the amazing benefits of publishing with this particular company was the author's compensation. He would be receiving *all the revenues* from book sales after the distributor had deducted their share!

I studied the contract, reviewed it with the author, asking many questions, and could find nothing wrong with it. I did ask the author to have the publishing company send him a marketing plan, but apparently they were unwilling to do so. They merely told him they were going to conduct an "aggressive campaign." That was the only red flag, but it was a big one. The term "aggressive" is meaningless unless accompanied by a document that spells out exactly what the publisher plans to do, how much money they intend to invest and how they plan to do it (with a time line).

Shortly afterward, I edited an exceptionally long manuscript for a client. Since it was a textbook and not what is called by the industry a "trade book" or product for general consumption, the length was permissible.

After I'd completed editing the work, my client asked if Dandelion would publish it. She was eager to get top sales for it; in fact, she even envisioned it as a best seller. Of course, she wanted to see it on the shelves of the brick & mortar bookstores.

I don't like to disillusion an author because I could always be wrong. Let's say I was 99% positive that this book did not fit best seller requirements. First of all, it was an esoteric book that had the potential for being banned or censored by some religious groups. Second, even if censorship would work in favor of delivering sales from the curious and clueless, these individuals would find her book difficult to read. I mentioned previously that it would be classified as a textbook.

It was not a trade book. It was not for the general public. Any book that will probably not appeal to the masses usually has little potential for hitting the best seller lists, or even for getting top sales. Clearly, my client had not visualized her readership when she listed her goals for this book—nor, for that matter, when she set out to write it.

I told my client it was an exceptional book; that was true and I felt honored to have had an opportunity to edit it. However, I told her frankly that I didn't see how my publishing company could get many sales for it because the work had such a select (and narrow) readership. Also, since we print our books digitally (print on demand), brick & mortar bookstores wouldn't sell it.

I suggested she send her manuscript to the "amazing publishing company" whose publishing contract I had just reviewed. It seemed to answer all her needs, and the price was certainly right.

She did as I suggested, but—here's the clincher—the "deal" they offered her was considerably different from the one that was given to the man whose contract I'd reviewed. She was asked to purchase 1,000, not 500 copies, and they asked her cut the book size in half. If she didn't want to do that work herself, they would do it, for a fee. Also, she would not receive all the revenues from sales. Again, no marketing plan was forthcoming, yet the word "aggressive" was included in her conversation with the company's director.

I was puzzled by the discrepancy in the two publishing contracts, so I contacted the man who had consulted with me.

Following is the information I did NOT know until then:

The publisher was in fact doing a first print run of 1000, but one of the man's clients who was a long-time best-selling author with this publisher, was paying for half the books, or 500 copies. This meant the man only had to buy the other 500. The celebrity author planned to give away those 500 books to his fan club. (Did you note that? Did you also note that this client is a best-selling author? I forgot to mention that he is also a marketing professional and a member of the National Speakers Bureau.) This promotion plan already gave the man a head start for his sales, since the best-selling author's fan club included some heavy-duty marketing people (in addition to himself) who, the publisher was well aware, would get behind the book and promote it through all of their own venues.

I don't know yet if this story has a happy ending, since the book was just published, but the "profit" question for the publisher was easily solved. The publishing company was making so much money on their celebrity author's books, they could afford to give his friend a good deal—especially if that celebrity author made a commitment to buy the first 500 copies and do some significant marketing and promotion for it himself.

As this book goes to press, I did learn that the publishing company has done no online marketing and promotion for the book. Although the author has a website, he was not informed that it might be a good idea to promote (and sell) the book on that site. He is not particularly computer savvy and knows nothing about social networking and online promotion strategies. Apparently the publisher doesn't consider online marketing particularly important, so it was not included in their "aggressive marketing campaign."

Since the book was written to support this practitioner's desire to enhance his client base, both offline in his physical office, and online through teleconferencing, in my humble opinion (IMHO) I believe it would surely be in his best interest to link his website to the book.

The reason for citing this example is not to try to find fault with this particular publisher, but to urge you to research your publishing choices carefully. Ask questions. Get definite answers. If someone is getting a better deal than you, as in this case, find out why. Be a good detective.

7 – Bottom Line

Self-publish and keep the lion's share of the profits

A couple years ago I started to advise my clients to self-publish, or open their own publishing companies, rather than publish with Dandelion. I wasn't trying to shoot myself in the foot; I just needed to be honest. I sincerely felt they would make more money and have more control of their project if they self-published.

It is indeed a fact that if you open your own publishing company you'll make the most money from book sales. You will sell your books through the print on demand system, with no intermediary distributors or wholesalers taking 60% of the profits. You will have the benefit of by-passing warehousing or inventory and fulfillment fees.

I suggest publishing your books in both hard copy and ebook formats. Invest in a website—one that you or your staff can design and build yourself.

Build a website with SiteSell (SBI!)

Build a website with SiteSell, (http://www.sitesell.com/publishing8.html). The founder of SiteSell, Dr. Ken Evoy, is a genius. SiteSell or SiteBuildIt! is by far the best bargain on the Internet and is guaranteed to give you less headaches than any other web building program.

I'm still almost computer illiterate, since I've focused 99% of my attention on the content part of the book industry: writing, doctoring and editing books. However, with the little knowledge I have about web design and html (the code used for writing web pages), I've created over 200 SBI! pages for my two websites, http://www.write-to-publish-for-profit.com and http://dandelion-books.com. The only help I received was development of the initial home page "look and feel" template.

For my first website, I also had a certified SBI! professional complete the initial keyword search for me, since I didn't have any experience with Search Engine Optimization (SEO). I did all the keyword development thereafter, which was easy because SBI! provides user friendly templates and clear instructions.

To build a web page, all you have to do is follow the instructions and adjust the page content according to the SBI! "analysis" check list.

Ken Evoy provides every tool you need for designing, building and maintaining your website. He also shows you how to pre-sell, get traffic and link the site to social networking, video, audio, etc. SBI!'s support manuals are great and so are their forums. Believe me, even if you don't know anything about building a website, you'll have a great experience with SBI!.

One other bonus: SBI! is an affiliate business. If you like to market online, this can be another side business. SBI! also provides mountains of support materials for showing you how to be a successful affiliate marketer.

If you don't have the time or inclination to build and maintain your own website and your business doesn't have its own IT team, you can contract the services of certified SBI! staff to do the work for you. Their rates are extremely reasonable—much lower cost than most web design and development companies. And, as I mentioned previously, you'll have the satisfaction of knowing the website is built for monetization.

Bottom line: If you build your website yourself with SBI! instead of contracting a professional company to do it, you will be fully empowered to make all changes and revisions yourself. You can easily update the pages. If you've ever paid someone to do this type of work, you know the fees can be whopping just for minor adjustments that you could have easily done yourself if your websites were SBI! self-built.

Professional web design and development companies do a great job, if they also build marketing into the website at the outset. That's a big "if." I built six websites with different companies and paid thousands of dollars for their services until I finally "got it," i.e., that I wouldn't have a functional website that attracted attention from the search engines until the keyword identification was properly built into each page… and until each page was developed according to SEO and keyword specifications.

I may take the gold medal for having built more non-functional websites than anyone in business… but maybe not. I'm well aware that thousands of people have been through the learning curve on building and maintaining websites and blogs.

Although my websites do not look like Silicon Valley masterpieces, I know their content has value. I also know the pages are written to reflect my personality, my values and what I want to tell the public and potential clients about my products and services.

Build an online empire

If your goal is to sell books and make a lot of money, it can be done. Make sure you consult with knowledgeable gurus. Like every industry, the Internet is filled with "questionable wannabees"; you may have already learned that.

You will need to build into your website the following:
- Blog
- Videos
- Audios
- Newsletter
- Social networking blog setup, including YouTube and other video blog spots

- Linked social networking groups
- Forums
- Article placement
- RSS Feeds

Your primary goal is to build a large opt-in email list for return customers. Learn how to build a squeeze page to sell your separate products, and diversify. Sell CDs and DVDs; harvest each of your products in several different formats.

Create joint ventures with friends and colleagues in order to build your email list. Network as much as possible.

You cannot possibly do all this yourself. Either hire a staff or go to a website such as guru.com to request help from the thousands of freelancers who do that type of work. Contract with a few of the experts. Remember to pay them well; they'll be loyal and do good work if they receive good pay.

Asking a writer to develop articles for $1.00 an article is unreasonable just as it is unreasonable to ask them to develop 50 articles in a week. The same holds true for blog and newsletter writing. Don't skimp or you'll end up with shoddy work. And remember... the key to success is having:

- Quality products to sell
- Quality customer service

- A quality business staff
- Quality business management procedures, and...

BEING A QUALITY PERSON

8

More About Marketing Your Books Online

Almost every day a new book or another online marketing guru appears with yet another Success Formula or end-all CD or DVD, with success stories to back up their products.

I've lost count of how many books and articles I've read on the subject, and how many tools and techniques I've tucked away in my mind or archived on my computer.

The fact is:

There is no one way because ultimately what will work for you may not work for anyone else. Or, what works for everyone else may not work for you.

The reason for this soon becomes obvious. Each of us is unique and we have a unique way of presenting ourselves and our material.

On the other hand:

Many of the success formulas for marketing and selling your book could make you a multi-millionaire overnight. You could make so much money simply following the step-by-step process outlined in a marketing expert's seminars or home study courses, you wouldn't hesitate to recommend this person's amazing program to everyone!

How can we know what's going to work for us without making a huge investment in many different marketing products and seminars?

Here's a check-off list of ToDo's:

- ✓ Review the contents of your book.
- ✓ Determine your target market. Who is your readership, or who will benefit most from buying and reading this book?
- ✓ What is the profile of your target market? For example, are they environmentally conscious? Spiritually oriented? Focused mainly on traditional values? College-age? Teenage? Single? Married? Entrepreneurially inclined? All of these?

The more clearly you can identify your target market, the easier it will be to determine what type of marketing will work best for your book.

For example, if your target market is young people and professionals who may do a lot of text messaging, your book will be a perfect candidate for viral marketing, social networking, blog development, etc.

You CAN do it!

You may always remember the first time someone you don't know—not your Aunt Susan or your sister or grandmother, but a total stranger—clicks on the "Buy Now" button and orders one of your books. It's a triumphant moment, and even if you've been strategically building a website, sales and promotion pages and doing everything possible to get the traffic snowballing, when it finally happens, you'll find yourself shaking your head in amazement.

That voice inside yelps excitedly, "Internet marketing actually works!!"

I remember back in the early nineties crowding around a computer while an Internet marketing expert brought up a tiny black and white photo of a wrist watch. Jubilantly he informed us that one day it would be possible to sell almost anything on the Internet.

Who would be the magician, we wondered. At the time there was no way for anyone to find the wrist watch, learn more about it, pay for it, and arrange to have it shipped.

That was only a few years ago.

In the late 90s, I ghostwrote and published a book for a company that was selling rejuvenation products and services. Amazon was so new, most people had never heard of it. When I told my colleagues that I'd placed their newly published book in an online bookstore, they thought I was crazy.

Who would ever go to a website to buy books, they joked. Why should they, when they could drive over to a Barnes & Noble or Borders, pick up whatever they wanted and carry it home with them? Instant gratification versus waiting for a book to be shipped seemed to be a much better option.

How times have changed!

Consider today the cost of gasoline, parking meter or parking lot fees; the time, energy and inconvenience of driving to a shopping mall or plaza to buy a book when you can sit down at your computer and in a matter of minutes order your book and have it drop shipped to your doorstep, often free of charge. (If you want it

8 – More About Marketing Your Books Online

shipped overnight, you may be happy to pay extra for that service.)

Today most of us are acutely aware that brick & mortar bookstores are having serious financial problems. The large chain establishments have resorted to becoming mini department stores that stock stationary, candles, toys, games, bath salts, aromatherapy, etc., AND books. Most of these stores also sell beverages and pastries.

Online bookselling has become a billion dollar industry. Print on demand digital technologies are rapidly replacing archaic offset printing, warehousing and distribution procedures. Direct marketing delivers most of the profits first to the author and publisher. Cutting out intermediaries has created a much more desirable business model.

We now know the power of the World Wide Web, Google, Yahoo, Bing, and other search engines. We also know that many people have been able to quit their day jobs and make sizable monthly incomes on the Internet.

Hard copy books that are printed "on demand" are an excellent product to sell from your website if you're willing to stock and ship them yourself.

Advantages: You'll make more money than selling them through Amazon.com, bn.com, Ebay and other online stores.

Disadvantages: Packing, picking and shipping require person power. At first, if your web traffic is small, this may not be a problem. However, as your business grows, it can be a chore. If you're selling several books, you will also need storage space.

In addition, you may feel that it's necessary to get a toll-free ordering number. This requires personnel to answer the phones if the orders start to come in thick and fast.

Another challenge is competition from established online stores. Possibly they offer discounts that you can certainly match, but if they also offer free shipping, after you've deducted the printing cost, your own shipping costs from the print on demand company to your office, and cost of both shipping materials and postal fees (plus labor, unless you want to offer your own labor free of charge), whatever's left may not seem worth it.

An excellent option is to sell your books through online stores such as amazon.com, alibris.com and bn.com. Join their affiliate programs and use your affiliate-embedded link whenever you promote your books from websites, blogs, lenses and other places. The online bookstores will stock your book (charging your print-on-demand company for the printing cost only when a book is sold) and do the picking, packing and shipping. Of course they'll charge for these services, but it will be worth it in the long run when you get into volume sales.

Experiment with Online Joint Ventures

When you include a joint venture in your book marketing campaign, you add value to the customer's order without asking them to pay more for your book.

Everyone loves bonuses; the word "free" is magical and can also imply specialness—you the seller are giving us the buyers a special deal. Why? Because we're smart (and special) enough to be here at the right time and place. And why are we *really* special? Because we chose to buy your book.

Subconsciously, the feeling of obtaining anything "free"—no strings attached—may also give us permission to do or be something or someone more than we would ordinarily be willing to commit to or believe in.

"Free" allows us to take risks. We take off the mufflers of inhibition and blast the world as loudly as we can: "FREE! FREE! FREE! Count me in! Don't leave me behind!"

Joint ventures have a carnival air about them. Lots of fun and excitement, big crowds and everyone spreading the word ABOUT YOUR BOOK.

For you, the author/entrepreneur/therapist, all this high energy floats upward and outward. Expansion broadens your playing field by adding potential opt-in email subscribers to your list. Several of those lists can total in the tens of thousands and deliver many more sales than anticipated.

Joint ventures build a community of colleagues supporting each other's endeavors.

How the JV works

Let's say Sally, a marriage and family counselor, has an ebook on time management for working parents with young children. You are a hypnotherapist and your book is about releasing stress. Your two books are a wonderful match. You suggest to Sally that she offer a free excerpt of her ebook as part of your list of buying incentives.

In your sales sheet or squeeze page, you will include a brief promotion paragraph for Sally's book, a photo of Sally and a hyperlink for downloading her free ebook excerpt.

Sally's autoresponder page where your buyers will download her free bonus may contain promotional material about her consulting services. It may also promote her new DVD on parenting, or other books and products she's developed.

Sally will support your joint venture by sending out a promotional email to her opt-in emailing list. The hidden message is: if these opt-in email subscribers respect Sally, they will trust her judgment in recommending the products and services of her colleagues.

This message is often right on target, and that's the beauty of joint ventures. Several people on Sally's list will subscribe to your site and possibly buy your book.

Every time you add other bonus or joint venture partner to your sales campaign, you multiply your potential for shoppers (and buyers).

You agree to support each other's sales campaigns by offering a free item to each of your squeeze pages. Joint ventures have joint benefits. In addition to boosting the campaign by offering buying incentives, joint ventures also provide free publicity for the generous donor.

Whenever the buyer accepts a joint venture partner's free gift (after making the purchase, of course), they will land on that partner's autoresponder downloading or shopping cart page.

Behind the scenes, you or your webmaster will have worked out the logistics of offering a commission to each of these joint venture partners whenever a sale comes in through one of their opt-in subscribers.

If you need help creating a joint venture, contact one or more of your favorite Internet marketing gurus and they'll be happy to refer you to the company they use. Or if they've developed their own joint venture software, you may be able to purchase it (after you subscribe to their opt-in email list!).

Check out the websites of some of the most successful Internet marketers. If you join their email subscription list and copy their procedures, you will know exactly how to include a joint venture in your book marketing campaign.

Membership Sites

You already have a membership site once people have subscribed to your opt-in email. Your site would be considered a public one or open to everyone.

A different type of membership site may charge an entry fee and block off a special section "for members only." The goal is to create an online "home" for the paying subscribers and to encourage these members to "come home" to this website daily or at least several times a week.

To maintain a private website, the owner makes a commitment to post new articles, blog entries, responses to members' feedback commentary, and other fresh material almost daily.

Attrition rate tends to be high for sites of this nature; people will join and participate for awhile. Then at a certain point, if the material starts to repeat itself or if it doesn't hold their interest, they'll unsubscribe and look elsewhere.

In some ways, this type of membership site is similar to a group therapy session. It works exceptionally well for people who like to air their problems publicly, and also for those who are looking for online companionship. Free social networking sites often work just as well for these people.

On a much higher level are private member sites run by competent professionals. A typical model is a blog run by a well-known journalist on the Beltway (Washington, D.C. area). He manages to get scoops almost daily, so his material is always juicy. Members are only too happy to pay a fee to read it. This type of blog is also perfect for selling books.

Some private membership sites do not charge a fee. For security or other proprietary reasons, the owners do not wish to welcome the public. Obviously these sites exist for information only, and would be categorized non-commercial.

You now have all the tools you need to write, publish and market your articles and books on the Internet.

If all of this seems like too much trouble...

You don't have to do any of it. You don't have to promote your published book at all, if you don't want to.

If you own a trucking business, a bicycle repair shop, bed and breakfast, organic fruit and veggie store, you don't have to necessarily build an online business for selling your book. Other online services may be listing your business in their directories and this may be sufficient for you to get noticed.

> Remember: your book is ALWAYS important as an introduction to you and your business. How you choose to publish, promote and distribute it is a personal matter.

I feel as though I've only started to cover the bases; there's so much more I could tell you... and by the time you read this section about marketing your book online, much of it may already be outdated.

I do know, however, that when you decide to write your own book, you will have one of the most exciting and exhilarating rides of

8 – More About Marketing Your Books Online

your life! In more ways than you can possibly imagine, your book will open doors for you: both inner and outer.

Try it, and see.

Do You Really Need To Write A Book?

I'm Here for You

If I can help you ghostwrite, book doctor or edit your book, let me know. I'll also be happy to consult with you concerning your publishing, distribution, marketing and promotion questions.

Wherever you live on Planet Earth, I am only a skype call or web cam away!

I can be reached by:

>info@caroladler.com
>www.caroladler.com
>www.write-to-publish-for-profit.com
>www.dandelion-books.com
>http://www.google.com/profiles/103054871135416190401

>Tel. 480-452-9183
>Fax 866-787-1972
>Skype ID – dandelionbooks

About the Author

Carol Adler, MFA's first ghost-written book listing her name as co-editor, *Why Am I Still Addicted? A Holistic Approach to Recovery*, was endorsed by Deepak Chopra, M.D., and published by McGraw-Hill. Other publications include three books on writing, publishing and marketing; three novels, four books of poetry; and well over 200 poems and short stories in literary journals. She has ghostwritten over 40 non-fiction and fiction works for a number of professionals in the education, health care and human potential industries.

Carol is President of Dandelion Books, LLC, (www.dandelion-books.com) of Mesa, Arizona; a full service 10-year-old publishing company. She is also President and CEO of Dandelion Enterprises, Inc., www.write-to-publish-for-profit.com and President of the International Arts & Media Foundation, a non-profit subsidiary of Dandelion Enterprises, Inc.

Her business experience includes co-ownership of a Palm Beach, FL public relations company and executive management positions in two U.S. rejuvenation and mind/body wellness corporations, for which she founded publishing divisions.

Carol has served as editor of several poetry and literary magazines. Her career experience includes extensive teaching of college-level creative and business writing, and conducting of writing workshops in prisons, libraries, elementary, junior and high schools, and senior citizen centers.

Testimonials from Carol's Clients

I have published three books with Dandelion Books (*Living with Soul*, volumes 1 & 2, and *It's All About Control*) and am delighted with their professionalism, attention to detail and willingness to work with authors. Carol Adler, the publisher, is a very easy person to work with and is dedicated to showcasing her authors' work on the Dandelion and other web sites, through book wholesalers and via a program of press releases.

Dandelion also uses cutting edge technology to present authors' works as e-books and is currently ramping up to a whole new set of e-book formats and outlets.

Tony Stubbs
Author, Book Production Expert
Radio Show Host
www.tjpublish.com

~ooOOoo~

The multi-talented Carol Adler, President of Dandelion Books, is so highly respected, gifted and knowledgeable that when I put a manuscript in her hands I know it will come back in ready to go condition. As a Professional Author of twelve books and counting with a busy speaking, training and writing career, I confess I don't have time for the painstaking wordsmithing or the patience to go over every little edit. With my work in Carol's capable hands I don't have to! I can confidently trust that my work (to the word!) will be perfectly turned out and polished to a very high standard. And that leaves me free to create the content I am purposeful and passionate about.

—Patricia Chamberlin
Author, Marketing Expert
Bio-Feedback Specialist, Entrepreneur
SuccessKey Publications, www.successkey.com

When it comes to book doctoring and editing, Carol Adler is that rare breed of technician and artist. She has the uncanny ability to get inside the author's own thoughts and feelings, pull out what is essential, and convert what is (often!) grammatical gibberish into powerful prose that reflects the author's unique individuality. I heartily recommend her for projects large and small, and tomes of all subject matter. Carol's awesome!

—Stephen Banick, MBA
Founder, The Gulliver Project, Inc.
Entrepreneur, Speaker, Catalyst
www.thegulliverproject.com ,www.superglobalcareers.com

~ooOOoo~

Thank you, Carol. You have guided me to where I am today. One of these days I will discipline myself to really watch my punctuation. Don't give up on me. I WILL get around to it eventually!

Keep in touch. Carol I have never met anyone quite like you. You are truly unique.

—Sheila LeSeuer, Author
Retired R.N. (Jersey Isle born WWII Survivor)

~ooOOoo~

Testimonials from Carol's Clients

I'd like to share my wonderful experience with Dandelion Press. I was referred to Carol Adler by Peter Shepherd of www.trans4mind.com. He is a European psychiatrist/therapist who runs several publications as well as a private practice and creating wellness and self help programs. Because I had come to respect him so immensely, I chose to contact Carol when I was ready to self-publish.

Carol is not only exceptionally well educated but reads people very well. Her writing expertise and business sense provided a marvelous backdrop for my first experience in this realm. An avid reader and publisher of a few short articles, I was a "babe in the woods" regarding the publishing arena. It's obvious that Carol has tremendous experiences in this arena.

Her marketing sense helped to hone my writings. Haha! Even though it's at times difficult to release the "baby" for suggestions by others, her ideas and rewrites - always with my permission - made my book most enjoyable and readable. My original drafts were a bit "haughty" and that wasn't my intention in communicating. Carol was able to "see" me and my personality... and when I felt a need to change things to be a bit more myself, she was super. I don't know how she manages to keep her own ego at bay - because of her tremendous skill and love of her field - but she does it with class!

Carol is a writer and I've read two of her novels. There is an ease in her style of writing... and that carries over to her dealings with people. She has depth of spirit, an uncanny awareness of humanity, and the ability to be generous. Carol is a true professional and today that is such a joy!

I have to admit that Carol's suggestions were the parts most enjoyed by friends, neighbors, and family with whom I shared my work. It has been such a grand feeling to have something of myself in written form in hardcopy. My daughters have enjoyed my humor, small takes on wisdom, and "hopeful" stance in my book. I would tell you quite candidly and with much enthusiasm that Carol Adler with her publishing house will be a wonderful step for you in fulfilling your own personal goals.

—Becky Ruff Reed
Author, Entrepreneur
www.reedpersonalassistant.com

Do You Really Need To Write A Book?

As you must know the word "Cromaat" was and is the word that the mystery schools use to seal a wish or anything that was done...I always use it... I use it like I use so mot it be!! Or, is done!!!

... I know you were chosen to help me. I don't think, there are too many people in the publishing business who have the spiritual awareness that I can feel you have. That fact makes me feel good because I know you will enhance my story and not butcher it.

...I also want to tell you that I love the way you write... the easy way of expression in your narrations...

I have placed my trust in you and I know that you will do a great job. Not only because you are an experienced professional in these matters but also because I think you feel the same way I do.

I thank God for letting me to meet you, I would not feel comfortable If I had to be working with my story with someone else...

GOD BLESS YOU.

—Norma Pastor, Author
Entrepreneur, The Alchemist Group

~ooOOoo~

I checked with several self-publishing companies prior to signing with Dandelion Books. Since signing, I have been very pleased with Dandelion and Carol Adler in particular. She is honest, has been very helpful whenever I have questions, is always available, and has helped advertise my book. Since my book has been published, Feb. 2007, I have placed three orders which arrived within 7-10 days. A nice convenience is that I can order as many or as few books as I need. I would highly recommend Dandelion Books.

—Dolores Proiette, Certified Hypnotherapist
Past Life Regression Specialist, Author
http://arizona.hypnosishealingcenter.com/

Carol... this is it. I know that God is in charge of *Marrisingle,* and you too....there isn't a day that goes by that I don't thank God for the opportunity to meet you. Even if we only sell one copy, the journey has been so worth it.

Wishing you the warmest blessing over Easter, love you, Brenda

Stretching the Wings of Change

I saw myself as a bird; my wings were ready to test the strongest wind now! One afternoon while reading the newspaper, my (third eye) picked out an announcement about a writing and publishing seminar that as to be given in the Phoenix area. "What do you think?" I turned to Randy, who was seated next to me, reading another section of the paper, "You know it always means something when a newspaper article pops right out at me! Should I take that *Marrisingle* journal to this seminar and see if it's worth pursuing? Get a professional opinion?"

Embracing my excitement, Randy encouraged me, "Yes, yes. Go, Brenda!"

Pulling into the parking lot, there it was again, that magical feeling of excitement that I was connecting with someone or something very special.

Three women introduced themselves and one in particular caught my eye. Shivers ran down my spine, with goose bumps quickly forming; *I knew it was the connection to her.* After a break in the presentation, I went outside and grabbed my typed manuscript. Before going inside again, I spoke to God: *Well, here it is God, you've been pushing me, nagging me for awhile to get on with this, here I am, right where I am suppose to be, and I am giving to the right One. So I know from here, you'll take it where it's suppose to be, no hard feelings God, if it was just to reach me, I am ok with that too!*

Eagerly I gave it over to the One. Smiling, I approached her, petite and very pretty, and she stood ready with a warm smile and outreached hand. "Hello, I'm Carol Adler, Dandelion Books."

It was if she was waiting for me. I introduced myself, explained the contents of my manuscript and where I was at, and asked if she would mind giving me her professional opinion.

Within several days, Carol called me back and we met. She told me how important *Marrisingle* could be, how helpful this book could be others. She urged me to tell my story because it would be valuable for others to know about my journey.

—Brenda Frantz
Professional Social Worker, Certified Hypnotherapist
Counselor, Professional Mediator
Author, *Marrisingle: Growing From Chaos*

~ooOOoo~

Carol,

You are so special, everything that I have read so far is spot on. Wow! I love the intro. I doubt that there will be that much to change. You have captured my words, my heart and it has brought tears to my eyes. You are an artist and I am in awe of your gifts!

You always make it fun for me and help me to relax and I am in awe of your gift.

—Ronna McEldowney
Professional Educator, Early Development Expert
http://www.partnersinparenting.net/

~ooOOoo~

(From a well-known investigative reporter)

Carol will be publishing my first hard copy book on XXXXX as well as helping me publish an e-book called XXXXX . . . . Carol has been working fiercely for her whole life for a free press and freedom of speech . . . Thank you, Carol for all your hard work and your bravery.

—S. F.

~ooOOoo~

Testimonials from Carol's Clients

[After reading *Naked in Daylight, Jesus & The Tooth Fairy, Arioso:*]

Carol, your poems are magnificent. They are most thought-provoking and require time to read. Your life experiences provide insights and wisdom that is the property of very few people.

—John H. Brand, D.Min., J.D.
Author, Retired Minister, Business Executive

~ooOOoo~

It's hard to make good publishing decisions nowadays. I get so many compliments on the cover art and interior of both Dandelion-published books.

I told the group in clay Center that anyone wanting a book doctor, ghost writer, or quality publishing should contact Dandelion. Not everyone can afford to pay for such services, but those who can, should make good use of your expertise.

You are a gem of a woman, Carol Adler.

Much love,
Laurel

—Laurel Johnson
Author (*The Alley of Wishes, My Name is Esther Clara*)
Senior Reviewer, *Midwest Book Review*
http://laureljohnsonblogs.blogspot.com/

[*From Dan Callahan, director of The Last Resort Panama, for whom Carol has been doing some ghostwriting and editing... Dan prefaced his newsletter article with a statement about Carol and then copied one of Carol's recent articles posted in on selfgrowth.com about anorexia/bulimia into the newsletter.*]

Yesterday I mentioned that I would be sharing info from two people that I **respect and admire. I used the term credibility. When I think of Carol that is** the term that comes to mind. She has a long list of successes to her career. When it comes to professionalism Carol stands above the rest of the field. Her insights are right on target.

Do You Really Need To Write A Book?

Carol Adler has been nothing short of spectacular as a friend and advisor. I think Carol lives on her computer. I send an email within minutes I have an answer. Carol is the CEO of the publishing company Dandelion Books. You can look her up at www.dandelion-books.com Thank You Carol!

—Dan Callahan, Director, The Last Resort Panama
www.thelastresortpa.com

~ooOOoo~

...I'm just a few chapters in to reading your edits and I just have to stop and tell you what an outstanding job you have done. You totally get what I'm trying to convey and your use of works to better tell the story is fantastic. You actually brought tears to my eyes after reading the first chapter because I'm so excited that my thoughts are coming alive and I can see the future for this book. Thank you!

—Michelle Prince, Author, Human Potential Speaker
http://www.coachmichelleprince.com/

I feel very blessed that I have found you.

I can't tell you how many times over the past 20 years or so I have said, "Oh forget it! Who cares if I ever get this book written!" Yet every time something would happen that pulled me right back. Just last week I told my daughter that I was going to give it up. I told her I was tired of struggling alone to get it finished. I longed for someone who would see the value of what I had to offer. I needed someone else's faith because as Donne stated and I am paraphrasing "No man is an island unto himself." Yes, we all need someone to believe in us. That is why your desire to help me brought tears to my eyes and hope in my heart and a strong determination that this time I will get it done.

Your professional help is exactly what I needed.

Blessings,
Ann Jovicin, MA
"THE PRACTICAL PSYCHOTHERAPIST"
Psychotherapist - Seminar Leader
LifeSuccess Consultant
Mastermind Group Coach
www.MySuccessStrategies.com

You are just too good to pass up, lol. I am going over my e-book and making some additions and corrections.

I also got a glimpse of all your other many talents and expertise. Wow!!!! an author, a poet, a hypnotherapist, a publisher. Is there anything you can't do???

I am looking forward to doing business with you Carol.

Take care,

> Rhonda Rabow, B.A., F.L.E., MA.
> Psychotherapist & Author
> http://www.helpmehelpmerhonda.ca

Dear Carol,

Today I'm working on getting Heaven News together, and in the process I started reading your free ebook, *Writers, Authors, and Dreamweavers.*

Carol, I am so often turned off by what I read, but what you wrote turned me on. I am so impressed I could just hug you. You have validated many things I needed to hear validated:

- Analyze for Technique Only
- Aim for the Heart
- Emotional Energy
- Passion

I love your writing altogether, and the words you choose: Dish Pan Gold, Elbow Grease Club... The true stories you tell, your quotes – perfect. I wish I had the ads you use when I was teaching school! I haven't read it to the end yet, Carol, but, believe me, I got the gold.

Loving you,
Gloria

—Gloria Wendroff, Godwriter™ The Godwriting™ International Society of Heaven
www.heavenletters.org and www.godwriting.org

Carol,

I am very pleased with your service. I love you,

Sharka

Sharka Glat
Author, Metaphysician, Teacher

~ooOOoo~

(Book Doctoring and development into a hard copy and ebook):

Hi Carol!

Wow! We were going to wait till tomorrow to write you but we wanted to put an early morning smile on your face so we are writing at this time so you get it first thing in the morning!

We knew all along you were the one to work on our book! Sixth sense I guess! You did an outstanding job!! And very fast!! You even added a few of your own special things... outstanding!! Cathy and I couldn't be happier!!

Dave & Cathy Burdick
Real Estate Advisors, Financial Counselors
http://www.911trusts.com

~ooOOoo~

From Guru.com:

Carol was amazing. I had a time schedule and she delivered early. We set a price and she stuck with it. No hidden fees. She was wonderful to work with and talk to. I give Carol the highest recommendation possible!

Randi Shannon
Author, Nutritionist, Counselor
www.NewAgeOfBeauty.com

Notes

Notes

Do You Really Need To Write A Book?

www.ingramcontent.com/pod-product-compliance
Lightning Source LLC
Chambersburg PA
CBHW031632160426
43196CB00006B/388